HALF
Taste of Home
homemade

TASTE OF HOME BOOKS • RDA ENTHUSIAST BRANDS, LLC • MILWAUKEE, WI

COVER PHOTOGRAPHER: Dan Roberts
COVER FOOD STYLIST: Lauren Knoelke
COVER SET STYLIST: Dee Dee Schaefer
PICTURED ON FRONT COVER: Easy Cheddar Chicken Potpie, p. 213
PICTURED ON BACK COVER: Saucy Chicken & Tortellini, p. 210;
Banana Cream Chocolate Truffles, p. 238; Swiss & Caraway
Flatbreads, p. 115
PICTURED ON TITLE PAGE: Shortcut Coconut-Pecan Chocolate
Tassies, p. 253
PICTURED ON SPINE: Caribbean Bread Pudding, p. 242

TITLE BANNER: pa3x/Shutterstock
TITLE LETTERING: Very_Very/Shutterstock

© 2018 RDA Enthusiast Brands, LLC
1610 N. 2nd St., Suite 102, Milwaukee WI 53212-3906

INTERNATIONAL STANDARD BOOK NUMBER: 978-1-61765-796-2
LIBRARY OF CONGRESS CONTROL NUMBER: 2018939397

Printed in China
1 3 5 7 9 10 8 6 4 2

ROSEMARY
CHEDDAR
MUFFINS, 80

CONTENTS

DAD'S FAVORITE BARBECUE
MEAT LOAVES, 173

FROZEN STRAWBERRY
DESSERT, 246

COLORFUL SPIRAL
PASTA SALAD, 139

SALMON PARTY
SPREAD, 40

LIKE US
facebook.com/tasteofhome

TWEET US
twitter.com/tasteofhome

FOLLOW US
@ tasteofhome

PIN US
pinterest.com/taste_of_home

SHOP WITH US shoptasteofhome.com
SHARE A RECIPE tasteofhome.com/submit

LOADED TATER
TOT BAKE, 36

Dishes that WOW without the work!

You really can cook great comfort foods and special treats—with less work than you ever imagined. Say hello to effortless meal prep with *Taste of Home Half Homemade!*

Great cooks: Even when crunched for time, they put fantastic home-cooked meals on the table. They consistently bring the winning potluck dishes that folks clamor for, and you can always count on them to be gracious hosts.

And now you can join their ranks—the easy way—when you cook from this ingenious recipe collection! Each dish uses shortcut ingredients to create authentic homemade taste, but with less prep time, fewer ingredients and foolproof results.

These are the recipes great home cooks love to share—and you will, too. From fun and fancy *Birthday Cake Waffles (p. 28)* to old-fashioned *Frozen Strawberry Dessert (p. 246)*, you can make any day memorable with a gorgeous treat.

And there are dozens of recipes for comforting soups, homey casseroles and great snacks you will be proud to serve. You'll wonder how you got by without these fabulous timesavers!

EASY NUTELLA
CHEESECAKE, 226

PESTO PULL-APART
BREAD, 103

SOUTHWESTERN
FISH TACOS, 158

Throughout the book, these **At-a-Glance** Icons make it easy to find recipes that fit your busy schedule.

Q Quick dishes are table-ready in just 30 minutes or less.

SC Slow-cooked recipes simmer while you work or play.

HASH BROWN PANCAKES
WITH SMOKED SALMON
& DILL CREAM, 15

CHAPTER 1

BEAUTIFUL BRUNCH DISHES

Good mornings are guaranteed thanks to luscious sweet rolls, elegant breakfasts and coffeehouse specialties...all made easy!

ⓠ EGG BASKETS BENEDICT

A little puff pastry turns Canadian bacon and eggs into a tasty update on eggs Benedict. We use a packaged hollandaise or cheese sauce for the finish.
—*Sally Jackson, Fort Worth, TX*

TAKES: 30 min. • **MAKES:** 1 dozen (1 cup sauce)

1 sheet frozen puff pastry, thawed
12 large eggs
6 slices Canadian bacon, finely chopped
1 envelope hollandaise sauce mix

1. Preheat oven to 400°. On a lightly floured surface, unfold puff pastry. Roll into a 16x12-in. rectangle; cut into twelve 4-in. squares. Place in greased muffin cups, pressing gently onto bottoms and up sides, allowing corners to point up.

2. Break and slip an egg into center of each pastry cup; sprinkle with Canadian bacon. Bake 10-12 minutes or until the pastry is golden brown, the egg whites are completely set and yolks begin to thicken but are not hard. Meanwhile, prepare hollandaise sauce according to package directions.

3. Remove pastry cups to wire racks. Serve warm with hollandaise sauce.

1 PASTRY CUP WITH 1 TBSP. SAUCE: 237 cal., 15g fat (6g sat. fat), 201mg chol., 355mg sod., 14g carb. (1g sugars, 2g fiber), 10g pro.

ⓢ SLOW COOKER SAUSAGE & WAFFLE BAKE

Here's an easy dish guaranteed to create excitement at the breakfast table.
Nothing is missing from this sweet and savory combination. It's so wrong, it's right!
—*Courtney Lentz, Boston, MA*

PREP: 20 min. • **COOK:** 5 hours + standing • **MAKES:** 12 servings

2 lbs. bulk spicy breakfast pork sausage
1 Tbsp. rubbed sage
½ tsp. fennel seed
1 pkg. (12.3 oz.) frozen waffles, cut into bite-sized pieces
8 large eggs
1¼ cups half-and-half cream
¼ cup maple syrup
¼ tsp. salt
¼ tsp. pepper
2 cups shredded cheddar cheese
Additional maple syrup

1. Fold two 18-in.-long pieces of foil into two 18x4-in. strips. Line the sides around the perimeter of a 5-qt. slow cooker with foil strips; spray with cooking spray.

2. In a large skillet, cook and crumble sausage over medium heat; drain. Add sage and fennel.

3. Place waffles in slow cooker; top with sausage. In a bowl, mix eggs, cream, syrup and seasonings. Pour over sausage and waffles. Top with cheese. Cook, covered, on low until set, 5-6 hours. Remove insert and let stand, uncovered, 15 minutes. Serve with additional maple syrup.

1 SERVING: 442 cal., 31g fat (12g sat. fat), 200mg chol., 878mg sod., 20g carb. (7g sugars, 1g fiber), 19g pro.

ⓠ FRUITY FRAPPE

Making a taste-alike of a restaurant drink is fun, but better yet, I know exactly what's in this one. My frappe gets its sweetness from berries, juice and honey.
—*Patty Crouse, Warren, PA*

TAKES: 10 min. • **MAKES:** 4 servings

1 cup water
1 cup fat-free milk
⅔ cup thawed orange juice concentrate
3 Tbsp. honey
½ tsp. vanilla extract
1 cup ice cubes
1 cup frozen unsweetened mixed berries

Place all ingredients in a blender; cover and process until blended. Serve immediately.

1¼ CUPS: 166 cal., 0 fat (0 sat. fat), 1mg chol., 28mg sod., 39g carb. (37g sugars, 1g fiber), 3g pro.

TEST KITCHEN TIP

The orange juice called for is half of a 12-ounce can of frozen concentrate. For best results, let it thaw overnight in the fridge. Mix the remaining concentrate with 1½ cans of water to make 3 cups of juice.

HASH BROWN PANCAKES WITH SMOKED SALMON & DILL CREAM

On weekends when I was growing up, pancakes, salmon and bagels were our brunch staples. I've combined the concepts and use whipped cream instead of cream cheese for a decadent finish.
—*Arlene Erlbach, Morton Grove, IL*

....

PREP: 15 min. • **COOK:** 20 min. • **MAKES:** 4 servings

⅓ cup heavy whipping cream

1⅛ tsp. dill weed, divided

4 cups frozen shredded hash brown potatoes, thawed

2 large eggs, beaten

2 Tbsp. minced chives

¼ tsp. salt

1 pkg. (3 to 4 oz.) smoked salmon or lox

1. Beat heavy whipping cream and 1 tsp. dill on high until stiff peaks form. Cover and refrigerate.

2. Preheat griddle over medium heat. Stir together potatoes, eggs, chives and salt until well combined. Grease griddle. Drop potato mixture by heaping ½ cupfuls onto griddle; flatten to ½-in. thick. Cook until bottoms are golden brown, about 10 minutes. Turn and cook until second sides are golden brown. Keep warm.

3. To serve, place salmon slices on pancakes. Top with whipped cream; sprinkle with remaining dill.

1 SERVING: 187 cal., 11g fat (6g sat. fat), 125mg chol., 350mg sod., 14g carb. (1g sugars, 1g fiber), 9g pro.

RED VELVET CINNAMON ROLLS

Turn red velvet cake mix into this delicious breakfast! The icing tastes like Cinnabon.
—*Erin Wright, Wallace, KS*

PREP: 20 min. + rising • **BAKE:** 15 min. • **MAKES:** 12 servings

1 pkg. red velvet cake mix (regular size)
2½ to 3 cups all-purpose flour
1 pkg. (¼ oz.) active dry yeast
1¼ cups warm water (120° to 130°)
½ cup packed brown sugar
1 tsp. ground cinnamon
¼ cup butter, melted

ICING
2 cups confectioners' sugar
2 Tbsp. butter, softened
1 tsp. vanilla extract
3 to 5 Tbsp. 2% milk

TEST KITCHEN TIP

Want 'em even more decadent? Instead of the glaze, spread a fluffy layer of cream cheese frosting over the top.

1. Combine the cake mix, 1 cup flour and yeast. Add water to dry ingredients; beat on medium speed for 2 minutes. Stir in enough remaining flour to form a soft dough (dough will be sticky). Turn onto a floured surface; knead gently 6-8 times. Place in a greased bowl, turning once to grease top. Cover and let rise in a warm place until doubled, about 2 hours. Mix brown sugar and cinnamon; set aside.

2. Punch down dough. Turn onto a lightly floured surface; roll dough into an 18x10-in. rectangle. Brush with melted butter to within ¼ in. of edges; sprinkle with sugar mixture.

3. Roll dough up jelly-roll style, starting with a long side; pinch seam to seal. Cut into 12 slices. Place in a greased 13x9-in. baking pan. Cover with a kitchen towel; let rise in a warm place until almost doubled, about 1 hour.

4. Preheat oven to 350°. Bake until puffed and light brown, 15-20 minutes. Cool slightly.

5. Beat confectioners' sugar, butter, vanilla and enough milk to reach a drizzling consistency. Drizzle icing over warm rolls.

1 CINNAMON ROLL: 429 cal., 10g fat (5g sat. fat), 16mg chol., 311mg sod., 81g carb. (48g sugars, 1g fiber), 5g pro.

EASY ORANGE ROLLS

Life on a dairy farm is busy, so I need breakfast recipes that are simple yet delicious. My teenage daughter has been helping in the kitchen for years. In fact, this was probably one of the first recipes she made herself.
—*Peggy Kraemer, Thief River, MN*

PREP: 15 min. • **BAKE:** 25 min. • **MAKES:** 16 servings

1 cup sugar
½ cup butter, cubed
¼ cup orange juice
2 Tbsp. grated orange zest
3 tubes (10 oz. each) refrigerated biscuits

1. In a small saucepan, combine the sugar, butter, orange juice and zest. Heat until sugar is dissolved and butter is melted. Pour into a greased 10-in. fluted tube pan.

2. Place 12 biscuits on their sides along the perimeter of the pan, overlapping slightly. Arrange remaining biscuits in the same manner, creating two concentric rings, using 10 biscuits for the middle ring and eight biscuits for the inside ring.

3. Bake at 350° for 25-30 minutes or until golden brown. Immediately turn upside down onto serving platter. Serve warm.

1 PIECE: 159 cal., 8g fat (4g sat. fat), 15mg chol., 226mg sod., 20g carb. (13g sugars, 0 fiber), 1g pro.

BREAKFAST SPUDS

Here's a dish that has it all—sweet potatoes, eggs, ham and cheese—for a powerful start to the day.
—*Annie Rundle, Muskego, WI*

TAKES: 30 min. • **MAKES:** 6 servings

1 pkg. (20 oz.) frozen sweet potato puffs
8 large eggs
⅓ cup 2% milk
¼ tsp. salt
⅛ tsp. pepper
1 cup cubed fully cooked ham
1 Tbsp. butter
Shredded cheddar cheese
Sliced green onions

1. Bake potato puffs according to package directions. In a large bowl, whisk eggs, milk, salt and pepper. Stir in ham.

2. In a large nonstick skillet, heat butter over medium heat. Add egg mixture; cook and stir until eggs are thickened and no liquid egg remains. Serve with potato puffs; sprinkle with cheese and green onions.

1 SERVING: 294 cal., 14g fat (4g sat. fat), 302mg chol., 752mg sod., 27g carb. (10g sugars, 2g fiber), 15g pro.

TEST KITCHEN TIP

For a Southern-inspired version, saute chopped green pepper, onion and andouille sausage before adding the eggs. Omit the ham. Season with cumin and paprika.

PUFF PASTRY DANISHES

Even though they're simple, these jam-filled pastries are right at home in a holiday brunch spread. They were my dad's favorite, so the recipe will always be close to my heart.
— *Chellie Richardson, Sidney, OH*

....

PREP: 30 min. • **BAKE:** 15 min. • **MAKES:** 1½ dozen

1 pkg. (8 oz.) cream cheese, softened
¼ cup sugar
2 Tbsp. all-purpose flour
½ tsp. vanilla extract
2 large egg yolks, divided
1 Tbsp. water
1 pkg. (17.3 oz.) frozen puff pastry, thawed
⅔ cup seedless raspberry jam or jam of choice
Additional sugar, optional

1. Preheat oven to 425°. Beat first four ingredients until smooth; beat in 1 egg yolk.

2. Mix water and remaining egg yolk. On a lightly floured surface, unfold each sheet of puff pastry; roll into a 12-in. square. Cut each into nine 4-in. squares; transfer to parchment paper-lined baking sheets.

3. Top each square with 1 Tbsp. cream cheese mixture and 1 rounded tsp. jam. Bring two opposite corners of pastry over filling, sealing with yolk mixture. Brush tops with remaining yolk mixture. If desired, sprinkle with additional sugar.

4. Bake until golden brown, 14-16 minutes. Serve warm. Refrigerate leftovers.

1 PASTRY: 197 cal., 12g fat (4g sat. fat), 33mg chol., 130mg sod., 20g carb. (3g sugars, 2g fiber), 3g pro.

FRUITY CROISSANT PUFF

I got this recipe from a good friend. Sweet, tart, tender and light, it tastes like a danish.
—*Myra Almer, Tuttle, ND*

PREP: 10 min. + chilling • **BAKE:** 45 min. • **MAKES:** 6 servings

4 large croissants, cut into 1-in. cubes (about 6 cups)
1½ cups mixed fresh berries
1 pkg. (8 oz.) cream cheese, softened
1 cup 2% milk
½ cup sugar
2 large eggs
1 tsp. vanilla extract
Maple syrup, optional

1. Place croissants and berries in a greased 8-in. square baking dish. In a medium bowl, beat cream cheese until smooth. Beat in milk, sugar, eggs and vanilla until blended; pour over croissants. Refrigerate unbaked casserole, covered, overnight.

2. Preheat oven to 350°. Remove casserole from refrigerator while oven heats.

3. Bake, covered, 30 minutes. Bake, uncovered, until puffed and golden and a knife inserted in the center comes out clean, 15-20 minutes more. Let stand for 5-10 minutes before serving. If desired, serve with maple syrup.

1 SERVING: 429 cal., 24g fat (14g sat. fat), 132mg chol., 358mg sod., 44g carb. (27g sugars, 2g fiber), 9g pro.

SAUSAGE CHEESE BISCUITS

These biscuits are a brunch favorite. I love that
they don't require any special ingredients.
—*Marlene Neideigh, Myrtle Point, OR*

TAKES: 30 min. • **MAKES:** 10 servings

1 tube (12 oz.) refrigerated buttermilk biscuits
1 pkg. (8 oz.) frozen fully cooked breakfast sausage links, thawed
2 large eggs, beaten
½ cup shredded cheddar cheese
3 Tbsp. chopped green onions

1. Preheat oven to 400°. Roll out each biscuit into a 5-in. circle; place each in an ungreased muffin cup. Cut sausages into fourths; brown in a skillet. Drain. Divide sausages among cups.

2. In a small bowl, combine eggs, cheese and onions; spoon into cups. Bake 13-15 minutes or until browned.

1 BISCUIT: 227 cal., 16g fat (6g sat. fat), 57mg chol., 548mg sod., 16g carb. (3g sugars, 0 fiber), 8g pro.

✳

DID YOU KNOW?

Cheddar gets its name from a village in England that is known for the delicious cheese.

BIRTHDAY CAKE WAFFLES

These super fun waffles—soft on the inside, crisp on the outside—
taste just like cake batter! They are quick to whip up anytime,
and they make birthday mornings feel even more special.
—Andrea Fetting, Franklin, WI

....

PREP: 20 min. • **COOK:** 25 min. • **MAKES:** 6 waffles

1 cup all-purpose flour
1 cup (about 5 oz.) confetti cake mix or flavor of choice
2 Tbsp. cornstarch
3 tsp. baking powder
¼ tsp. salt
2 Tbsp. rainbow sprinkles, optional
2 large eggs
1¾ cups 2% milk
¾ to 1 cup plain Greek yogurt
½ tsp. vanilla extract
½ tsp. almond extract

CREAM CHEESE FROSTING

4 oz. softened cream cheese or reduced-fat cream cheese
¼ cup butter, softened
1½ to 2 cups confectioners' sugar
½ tsp. vanilla extract
1 to 3 Tbsp. 2% milk

1. Preheat oven to 300°. Combine the first five ingredients and, if desired, rainbow sprinkles. In another bowl, whisk eggs, milk, yogurt and extracts. Add yogurt mixture to flour mixture; mix until smooth.

2. Preheat waffle maker coated with cooking spray. Bake waffles according to manufacturer's directions until golden brown. Transfer cooked waffles to oven until ready to serve.

3. For frosting, beat cream cheese and butter on high until light and fluffy, 2-3 minutes. Gradually beat in confectioners' sugar, ½ cup at a time, until smooth. Beat in vanilla. Add enough milk to reach desired consistency. Spread over warm waffles. For a cakelike look, cut waffles into fourths and stack them; decorate with birthday candles.

1 WAFFLE: 528 cal., 22g fat (13g sat. fat), 115mg chol., 695mg sod., 72g carb. (45g sugars, 1g fiber), 10g pro.

EGG-TOPPED WILTED SALAD

Tossed with a bright champagne vinegar dressing and topped with chipotle bacon and sunny eggs, this is the ultimate brunch salad. But it's so delicious I'd gladly enjoy it any time of day!
—*Courtney Gaylord, Columbus, IN*

PREP: 20 min. • **BAKE:** 25 min. • **MAKES:** 4 servings

8 bacon strips
1 tsp. packed brown sugar
¼ tsp. ground chipotle pepper
1 small red onion, halved and thinly sliced
2 Tbsp. champagne vinegar
1 tsp. sugar
½ tsp. pepper
4 large eggs
¼ tsp. salt
8 cups spring mix salad greens (about 5 oz.)
½ cup crumbled feta cheese

1. Preheat oven to 350°. Place bacon on one half of a foil-lined 15x10x1-in. pan. Mix brown sugar and chipotle pepper; sprinkle evenly over bacon. Bake until bacon begins to shrink, about 10 minutes.

2. Using tongs, move bacon to other half of pan. Add onion to bacon drippings, stirring to coat. Return to oven; bake until bacon is crisp, about 15 minutes. Drain on paper towels, reserving 2 Tbsp. drippings.

3. In a small bowl, whisk together vinegar, sugar, pepper and reserved drippings. Coarsely chop bacon.

4. Place a large nonstick skillet coated with cooking spray over medium-high heat. Break eggs, one at a time, into pan. Reduce heat to low; cook eggs until desired doneness, turning after whites are set if desired. Sprinkle with salt.

5. Toss the salad greens with dressing; divide among four plates. Top with bacon, onion, cheese and eggs. Serve immediately.

1 SERVING: 279 cal., 20g fat (8g sat. fat), 216mg chol., 730mg sod., 10g carb. (3g sugars, 3g fiber), 17g pro.

SIMPLE ICED COFFEE

My husband came up with this recipe to replace the soda he was drinking every morning. It's a delicious alternative to expensive iced coffees from the local cafe.
—*Sarah Lange, Watertown, WI*

TAKES: 5 min. • **MAKES:** 8 servings

2 cups water
¼ cup instant coffee granules
¼ to ½ cup sugar
4 cups 2% milk
2 cups half-and-half cream
2 tsp. vanilla extract or hazelnut flavoring syrup, optional

1. Microwave water 90 seconds. Stir in instant coffee. Add sugar.

2. Stir in milk, cream and, if desired, extract or flavoring until combined. Serve over ice.

1 CUP: 174 cal., 8g fat (6g sat. fat), 40mg chol., 88mg sod., 15g carb. (14g sugars, 0 fiber), 6g pro.

✱
TEST KITCHEN TIP

You can make this recipe an iced mocha by subbing chocolate milk for white. If desired, keep a coffee flavoring syrup on the side so each person can flavor their coffee accordingly. Orange-flavored syrup is another tasty option.

GRANDMOTHER'S TOAD IN A HOLE

I have fond memories of my grandmother's Yorkshire pudding wrapped around sausages, a puffy dish my kids called The Boat. Slather it with butter and maple syrup.
—*Susan Kieboam, Streetsboro, OH*

PREP: 10 min. + standing • **BAKE:** 25 min. • **MAKES:** 6 servings

3 large eggs
1 cup 2% milk
½ tsp. salt
1 cup all-purpose flour
1 pkg. (12 oz.) uncooked maple breakfast sausage links
3 Tbsp. olive oil
Butter and maple syrup, optional

1. Preheat oven to 400°. In a small bowl, whisk eggs, milk and salt. Whisk flour into egg mixture until blended. Let stand 30 minutes. Meanwhile, cook sausage according to package directions; cut each sausage into three pieces.

2. Place oil in a 12-in. nonstick ovenproof skillet. Place in oven 3-4 minutes or until hot. Stir batter and pour into prepared skillet; top with sausage. Bake 20-25 minutes or until golden brown and puffed. Remove from skillet; cut into wedges. If desired, serve with butter and syrup.

1 WEDGE: 336 cal., 22g fat (6g sat. fat), 126mg chol., 783mg sod., 20g carb. (2g sugars, 1g fiber), 14g pro.

LOADED TATER TOT BAKE

I keep frozen Tater Tots on hand for meals like this yummy casserole. It's a super brunch, breakfast or side dish for kids of all ages.
—*Nancy Heishman, Las Vegas, NV*

PREP: 15 min. • **BAKE:** 35 min. • **MAKES:** 6 servings

1 Tbsp. canola oil
1 medium onion, finely chopped
6 oz. Canadian bacon, cut into ½-in. strips
4 cups frozen Tater Tots, thawed
6 large eggs, lightly beaten
½ cup reduced-fat sour cream
½ cup half-and-half cream
1 Tbsp. dried parsley flakes
¾ tsp. garlic powder
½ tsp. pepper
1½ cups shredded cheddar cheese

1. Preheat oven to 350°. In a large skillet, heat oil over medium heat. Add onion; cook and stir 2-3 minutes or until tender. Add Canadian bacon; cook 1-2 minutes or until lightly browned, stirring occasionally. Remove from heat.

2. Line bottom of a greased 11x7-in. baking dish with Tater Tots; top with Canadian bacon mixture. In a large bowl, whisk eggs, sour cream, cream and seasonings until blended. Stir in cheese; pour over top. Bake, uncovered, 35-40 minutes or until golden brown.

1 PIECE: 443 cal., 29g fat (12g sat. fat), 243mg chol., 917mg sod., 23g carb. (4g sugars, 2g fiber), 22g pro.

SHEPHERD'S INN BREAKFAST PIE: Substitute 1½ pounds bulk pork sausage, cooked and drained, for onion and Canadian bacon. Substitute ¾ cup milk for the sour cream and cream; omit pepper. Assemble and bake as directed. Top with 2 chopped tomatoes.

APPLE-GOUDA PIGS
IN A BLANKET, 47

CHAPTER 2

PARTY-TIME CLASSICS

Whether it's a holiday potluck, family reunion or casual get-together, these simply delightful snacks and drinks let the good times roll.

SALMON PARTY SPREAD

We're proud to serve our delicious Alaskan salmon to guests. Set out some crackers, and this slightly smoky spread will be gone in no time!
—*Kathy Crow, Cordova, AK*

PREP: 10 min. + chilling • **MAKES:** 2 cups

1 pkg. (8 oz.) cream cheese, softened
1 can (7½ oz.) pink salmon, drained, flaked and cartilage removed
3 Tbsp. chopped fresh parsley
2 Tbsp. finely chopped green pepper
2 Tbsp. finely chopped sweet red pepper
2 tsp. lemon juice
1 tsp. prepared horseradish
½ tsp. liquid smoke, optional
   Finely chopped pecans and additional parsley, optional
   Crackers

In a bowl, combine the first eight ingredients; stir until well blended. Cover and chill two to 24 hours. Transfer to a serving bowl; if desired, sprinkle with pecans and parsley. Serve with crackers.

2 TBSP.: 71 cal., 6g fat (3g sat. fat), 21mg chol., 115mg sod., 1g carb. (0 sugars, 0 fiber), 4g pro.

DID YOU KNOW?

Wild salmon is 20% leaner than farm-raised and is higher in heart-healthy omega-3 fatty acids. The can label will indicate whether the salmon is wild or farmed. If it's marked "Altantic," it's farmed. Alaskan salmon, on the other hand, is wild-caught.

❶ REUBEN ROUNDS

Fans of the classic Reuben sandwich will go crazy for baked pastry spirals of corned beef, Swiss and sauerkraut. They're a breeze to make, and bottled Thousand Island dressing makes the perfect dipping sauce.
—*Cheryl Snavely, Hagerstown, MD*

TAKES: 30 min. • **MAKES:** 16 appetizers

1 sheet frozen puff pastry, thawed
6 slices Swiss cheese
5 slices deli corned beef
½ cup sauerkraut, rinsed and well drained
1 tsp. caraway seeds
¼ cup Thousand Island salad dressing

1. Preheat oven to 400°. Unfold puff pastry; layer with cheese, corned beef and sauerkraut to within ½-in. of edges. Roll up jelly-roll style. Trim ends and cut crosswise into 16 slices. Place on greased baking sheets, cut side down. Sprinkle with caraway seeds.

2. Bake 18-20 minutes or until golden brown. Serve with salad dressing.

1 APPETIZER: 114 cal., 7g fat (2g sat. fat), 8mg chol., 198mg sod., 10g carb. (1g sugars, 1g fiber), 3g pro.

❶ CHERRY-ALMOND TEA MIX

Our family enjoys giving homemade gifts for Christmas, and hot beverage mixes are especially popular. This flavored tea is a favorite.
—*Andrea Horton, Kelso, WA*

TAKES: 10 min. • **MAKES:** 40 servings (2½ cups tea mix)

2¼ cups iced tea mix with lemon and sugar

2 envelopes (0.13 oz. each) unsweetened cherry Kool-Aid mix

2 tsp. almond extract

EACH SERVING

1 cup boiling or cold water

Place tea mix, Kool-Aid mix and extract in a food processor; pulse until blended. Store in an airtight container in a cool, dry place for up to 6 months.

TO PREPARE TEA: Place 1 Tbsp. tea mix in a mug. Stir in 1 cup boiling or cold water until blended.

1 CUP PREPARED TEA: 41 cal., 0 fat (0 sat. fat), 0 chol., 1mg sod., 10g carb. (10g sugars, 0 fiber), 0 pro.

ⓠ APPLE-GOUDA PIGS IN A BLANKET

For New Year's, I used to make beef and cheddar pigs in a blanket, but now
I like apple and Gouda for an even better flavor celebration.
—*Megan Weiss, Menomonie, WI*

TAKES: 30 min. • **MAKES:** 2 dozen

1 tube (8 oz.) refrigerated crescent rolls
1 small apple, peeled and cut into 24 thin slices
6 thin slices Gouda cheese, quartered
24 miniature smoked sausages
Honey mustard salad dressing, optional

1. Preheat oven to 375°. Unroll crescent dough and separate into eight triangles; cut each lengthwise into three thin triangles. On the wide end of each triangle, place one slice of apple, one folded piece of cheese and one sausage; roll up tightly.

2. Place 1 in. apart on parchment paper-lined baking sheets, point side down. Bake until golden brown, 10-12 minutes. If desired, serve with dressing.

1 APPETIZER: 82 cal., 6g fat (2g sat. fat), 11mg chol., 203mg sod., 5g carb. (1g sugars, 0 fiber), 3g pro.

ANTIPASTO BAKE

Stuffed with savory meats and cheeses, this hearty bake would satisfy
an entire offensive line! It comes together quickly and bakes in under an hour,
making it the perfect potluck bring-along. There are so many all-stars in this
ooey-gooey appetizer. A crisp topping finishes it off.
—*Brea Barclay, Green Bay, WI*

PREP: 20 min. • **BAKE:** 45 min. + standing • **MAKES:** 20 servings

2 tubes (8 oz. each) refrigerated crescent rolls
¼ lb. thinly sliced hard salami
¼ lb. thinly sliced Swiss cheese
¼ lb. thinly sliced pepperoni
¼ lb. thinly sliced Colby-Monterey Jack cheese
¼ lb. thinly sliced prosciutto
¼ lb. thinly sliced provolone cheese
2 large eggs
½ tsp. garlic powder
½ tsp. pepper
1 jar (12 oz.) roasted sweet red peppers, drained
1 large egg yolk, beaten

1. Preheat oven to 350°. Unroll one tube of crescent dough into one long rectangle; press perforations to seal. Press onto bottom and up sides of an ungreased 11x7-in. baking dish.

2. Layer meats and cheeses on dough in the order listed. Whisk eggs and seasonings until well blended; pour into dish. Top with roasted pepper.

3. Unroll the remaining tube of dough into a long rectangle; press perforations to seal. Place over filling; pinch seams tight. Brush with beaten egg yolk; cover with foil. Bake for 30 minutes; remove foil. Bake until golden brown, 15-20 minutes. Let stand 20 minutes.

1 PIECE: 229 cal., 15g fat (7g sat. fat), 58mg chol., 662mg sod., 10g carb. (2g sugars, 0 fiber), 11g pro.

SLOW COOKER SPINACH & ARTICHOKE DIP

With this creamy dip, I can get my daughters to eat spinach and artichokes. We serve it with chips, toasted pita bread or fresh veggies.
—*Jennifer Stowell, Deep River, IA*

PREP: 10 min. • **COOK:** 2 hours • **MAKES:** 8 cups

2 cans (14 oz. each) water-packed artichoke hearts, drained and chopped

2 pkg. (10 oz. each) frozen chopped spinach, thawed and squeezed dry

1 jar (15 oz.) Alfredo sauce

1 pkg. (8 oz.) cream cheese, cubed

2 cups shredded Italian cheese blend

1 cup shredded part-skim mozzarella cheese

1 cup shredded Parmesan cheese

1 cup 2% milk

2 garlic cloves, minced
Assorted crackers and/or cucumber slices

In a greased 4-qt. slow cooker, combine the first nine ingredients. Cook, covered, on low for 2-3 hours or until heated through. Serve dip with crackers and/or cucumber slices.

¼ CUP: 105 cal., 7g fat (4g sat. fat), 21mg chol., 276mg sod., 5g carb. (1g sugars, 1g fiber), 6g pro.

TEST KITCHEN TIP

To make a fresh garlic clove easy to peel, gently crush it with the flat side of a large knife blade to loosen the peel. If you don't have a large knife, you can crush the garlic with a small can. The peel will come right off.

ⓠ EASY IRISH CREAM

Whip up this fast and easy recipe for a potluck brunch.
There's plenty of coffee flavor in every cozy cup.
—Anna Hansen, Park City, UT

TAKES: 15 min. • **MAKES:** 5 cups

2 cups half-and-half cream
1 can (13.4 oz.) dulce de leche or sweetened condensed milk
1¼ cups Irish whiskey
¼ cup chocolate syrup
2 Tbsp. instant coffee granules
2 tsp. vanilla extract
Hot brewed coffee or ice cubes

Pulse all ingredients in a blender until smooth. Stir 1-2 Tbsp. into a mug of hot coffee, or pour over ice.

½ CUP: 415 cal., 21g fat (13g sat. fat), 79mg chol., 116mg sod., 35g carb. (34g sugars, 0 fiber), 4g pro.

TOASTED HAZELNUT: Pulse 2 cups half-and-half cream, 1 can dulce de leche or sweetened condensed milk, 1¼ cups hazelnut liqueur and 2 Tbsp. instant coffee granules in a blender until smooth.

BUTTER MINT: Pulse 2 cups half-and-half cream, 1 can dulce de leche or sweetened condensed milk, 1¼ cups peppermint schnapps and 2 Tbsp. butter extract in a blender until smooth.

SALTED CARAMEL: Pulse 2 cups half-and-half cream, 1 can dulce de leche or sweetened condensed milk, 1¼ cups butterscotch schnapps and ¼ tsp. salt in a blender until smooth.

CHOCOLATE-COVERED CHERRY: Pulse 2 cups half-and-half cream, 1 can dulce de leche or sweetened condensed milk, 1¼ cups amaretto and ½ cup chocolate syrup in a blender until smooth.

ⓢ MEXICAN FONDUE

This irresistible fondue has become such a favorite with family and friends, I make it often for all kinds of occasions. It's fun to serve with fondue forks if you have them.
—*Nella Parker, Hersey, MI*

PREP: 15 min. • **COOK:** 1½ hours • **MAKES:** 4½ cups

1 can (14¾ oz.) cream-style corn
1 can (14½ oz.) diced tomatoes, drained
3 Tbsp. chopped green chilies
1 tsp. chili powder
1 pkg. (16 oz.) process cheese (Velveeta), cubed
  French bread cubes

1. In a small bowl, combine the corn, tomatoes, green chilies and chili powder. Stir in cheese. Pour mixture into a 1½-qt. slow cooker coated with cooking spray.

2. Cover and cook on high for 1½ hours, stirring every 30 minutes or until cheese is melted. Serve warm with bread cubes.

¼ CUP: 105 cal., 6g fat (4g sat. fat), 20mg chol., 421mg sod., 7g carb. (3g sugars, 1g fiber), 5g pro.

SLOW COOKER CHEESE DIP: Cook ½ pound ground beef and ¼ pound bulk spicy pork sausage; drain. Place in slow cooker with Velveeta and 1 can (10 oz.) diced tomatoes and green chilies. Cook as directed. Serve with tortilla chips.

HEARTY BROCCOLI DIP: Cook 1 pound ground beef; drain. Place in slow cooker with Velveeta, 1 can (10¾ oz.) condensed cream of mushroom soup, 3 cups frozen chopped broccoli (thawed) and 2 Tbsp. salsa. Cook as directed. Serve with tortilla chips.

SPINACH DIP IN A BREAD BOWL

When we get together with friends, I like to prepare this creamy dip. It's a crowd-pleaser.
—*Janelle Lee, Appleton, WI*

PREP: 15 min. + chilling • **MAKES:** 15 servings

2 cups sour cream
1 envelope (1 oz.) ranch salad dressing mix
1 pkg. (10 oz.) frozen chopped spinach, thawed and well drained
¼ cup chopped onion
¾ tsp. dried basil
½ tsp. dried oregano
1 round loaf of bread (1 lb.)
Raw vegetables

1. In a large bowl, combine first six ingredients. Chill for at least 1 hour. Cut a 1½-in. slice off the top of the loaf; set aside. Hollow out the bottom part, leaving a thick shell. Cut or tear the slice from the top of the loaf and the bread from inside into bite-size pieces.

2. Fill the shell with dip; set on a large platter. Arrange the bread pieces and vegetables around the bowl and serve immediately.

1 SERVING: 161 cal., 6g fat (4g sat. fat), 22mg chol., 571mg sod., 20g carb. (2g sugars, 1g fiber), 4g pro.

ⓈⒸ ASIAN PULLED PORK SANDWICHES

My pulled pork is a happy flavor mash-up of Vietnamese pho noodle soup and a banh mi sandwich. It's one seriously delicious slow cooker dish.
—*Stacie Anderson, Virginia Beach, VA*

PREP: 15 min. • **COOK:** 7 hours • **MAKES:** 18 servings

½ cup hoisin sauce
¼ cup seasoned rice vinegar
¼ cup reduced-sodium soy sauce
¼ cup honey
2 Tbsp. tomato paste
1 Tbsp. Worcestershire sauce
2 garlic cloves, minced
4 lbs. boneless pork shoulder roast
18 French dinner rolls (about 1¾ oz. each), split and warmed
Optional toppings: shredded cabbage, julienned carrot, sliced jalapeno pepper, fresh cilantro and/or basil and Sriracha Asian hot chili sauce

1. In a small bowl, whisk the first seven ingredients until blended. Place roast in a 4- or 5-qt. slow cooker. Pour sauce mixture over top. Cook, covered, on low 7-9 hours or until pork is tender.

2. Remove roast; cool slightly. Skim fat from cooking juices. Coarsely shred pork with two forks. Return pork to slow cooker; heat through. Using tongs, serve pork on rolls, adding toppings as desired.

FREEZE OPTION: Freeze cooled meat mixture in freezer containers. To use, partially thaw in refrigerator overnight. Heat through in a saucepan, stirring occasionally and adding a little broth if necessary. Serve as directed.

1 SANDWICH: 350 cal., 12g fat (4g sat. fat), 60mg chol., 703mg sod., 35g carb. (8g sugars, 1g fiber), 23g pro.

ⓠ FESTIVE APPLE DIP

I came up with this layered peanut butter treat when my dad gave me a big bag of apples. The dip has been one of my favorites ever since. In addition to serving it with apples, try it with graham crackers, vanilla wafers, banana chunks or animal crackers.
—*Theresa Tometich, Coralville, IA*

TAKES: 20 min. • **MAKES:** 8 servings

1 pkg. (8 oz.) cream cheese, softened
½ cup creamy peanut butter
⅓ cup packed brown sugar
1 tsp. vanilla extract
½ cup miniature marshmallows
1 jar (11¾ oz.) hot fudge ice cream topping
2 Tbsp. chopped mixed nuts or peanuts
3 each medium red and green apples, cut into thin wedges
2 Tbsp. lemon juice

1. For dip, beat first four ingredients until smooth; stir in marshmallows. Spoon half of the mixture into a 3-cup bowl; top with half of the fudge topping. Repeat layers. Sprinkle with nuts.

2. To serve, toss the apples with lemon juice. Serve with dip.

¼ CUP DIP WITH ¾ APPLE: 403 cal., 22g fat (9g sat. fat), 29mg chol., 218mg sod., 49g carb. (38g sugars, 3g fiber), 8g pro.

LUSCIOUS LIME SLUSH

Guests really go for this sweet-tart refresher. If you prefer, swap in lemonade concentrate for the limeade.
—*Bonnie Jost, Manitowoc, WI*

PREP: 20 min. + freezing • **MAKES:** 28 servings

9 cups water

4 individual green tea bags

2 cans (12 oz. each) frozen limeade concentrate, thawed

2 cups sugar

2 cups lemon rum or rum

7 cups lemon-lime soda, chilled

1. In a Dutch oven, bring water to a boil. Remove from the heat; add tea bags. Cover and steep for 3-5 minutes. Discard tea bags. Stir in the limeade concentrate, sugar and rum.

2. Transfer to a 4-qt. freezer container; cool. Cover and freeze for 6 hours or overnight.

TO PREPARE SLUSH: Combine the limeade mixture and lemon-lime soda in a 4-qt. pitcher. Or, for one serving, combine ½ cup limeade mixture and ¼ cup soda in a glass. Serve immediately.

¾ CUP: 177 cal., 0 fat (0 sat. fat), 0 chol., 7mg sod., 36g carb. (35g sugars, 0 fiber), 0 pro.

PROSCIUTTO PINWHEELS

These fancy appetizers are a lot easier to make than they look.
With just a few ingredients, they're a snap!
—*Kaitlyn Benito, Everett, WA*

PREP: 20 min. • **BAKE:** 15 min. • **MAKES:** 20 appetizers

1 sheet frozen puff pastry, thawed
¼ cup sweet hot mustard
¼ lb. thinly sliced prosciutto or deli ham, chopped
½ cup shredded Parmesan cheese

1. Unfold puff pastry. Spread mustard over pastry to within ½ in. of edges. Sprinkle with prosciutto and cheese. Roll up one side to the middle of the dough; roll up the other side so the two rolls meet in the center. Using a serrated knife, cut into ½-in. slices.

2. Place on greased baking sheets. Bake at 400° for 11-13 minutes or until puffed and golden brown. Serve warm.

FREEZE OPTION: Freeze cooled appetizers in freezer containers, separating layers with waxed paper. To use, reheat appetizers on a greased baking sheet in a preheated 400° oven until crisp and heated through.

1 SERVING: 86 cal., 5g fat (1g sat. fat), 6mg chol., 210mg sod., 8g carb. (0 sugars, 1g fiber), 3g pro. *Diabetic exchanges:* 1 fat, ½ starch.

ⓠ ASPARAGUS WITH HORSERADISH DIP

This is a terrific dip for party season. Serve asparagus on a decorative platter with lemon wedges on the side for garnish. For a flavor variation, use chopped garlic in place of the horseradish.
—*Lynn Caruso, Gilroy, CA*

TAKES: 15 min. • **MAKES:** 16 servings

32 fresh asparagus spears (about 2 lbs.), trimmed
1 cup reduced-fat mayonnaise
¼ cup grated Parmesan cheese
1 Tbsp. prepared horseradish
½ tsp. Worcestershire sauce

1. Place asparagus in a steamer basket; place in a large saucepan over 1 in. of water. Bring to a boil; cover and steam for 2-4 minutes or until crisp-tender. Drain and immediately place in ice water. Drain and pat dry.

2. In a small bowl, combine the remaining ingredients. Serve with asparagus.

2 ASPARAGUS SPEARS WITH 1 TBSP. DIP: 63 cal., 5g fat (1g sat. fat), 6mg chol., 146mg sod., 3g carb. (1g sugars, 0 fiber), 1g pro. *Diabetic exchanges:* 1 fat.

ⓠ MEXICAN DEVILED EGGS

My husband and I live on a beautiful lake and host lots of summer picnics and cookouts. I adapted this recipe to suit our tastes. Folks who are expecting the same old deviled eggs are surprised when they try this delightfully tangy variation.
—Susan Klemm, Rhinelander, WI

TAKES: 15 min. • **MAKES:** 8 servings

8 hard-boiled large eggs
½ cup shredded cheddar cheese
¼ cup mayonnaise
¼ cup salsa
2 Tbsp. sliced green onions
1 Tbsp. sour cream
Salt to taste

1. Slice the eggs in half lengthwise; remove yolks and set the whites aside. In a small bowl, mash yolks with cheese, mayonnaise, salsa, onions, sour cream and salt.

2. Spoon or pipe into egg whites. Serve immediately or chill until ready to serve.

2 FILLED EGG HALVES: 159 cal., 13g fat (4g sat. fat), 223mg chol., 178mg sod., 1g carb. (1g sugars, 0 fiber), 8g pro.

TEST KITCHEN TIP
Keep these appetizers from rolling around even if you don't have a deviled egg plate. Just cut a tiny slice from the outside of each egg half so it sits flat.

9-LAYER GREEK DIP

Instead of the same taco dip at every family event or potluck, try
this light, cool, refreshing alternative. It both looks and tastes healthy.
—*Shawn Barto, Winter Garden, FL*

TAKES: 20 min. • **MAKES:** 5½ cups

- 1 carton (10 oz.) hummus
- 1 cup refrigerated tzatziki sauce
- ½ cup chopped green pepper
- ½ cup chopped sweet red pepper
- ½ cup chopped peeled cucumber
- ½ cup chopped water-packed artichoke hearts, drained
- ½ cup chopped pitted Greek olives, optional
- ¼ cup chopped pepperoncini
- 1 cup crumbled feta cheese
  Baked pita chips

In a 9-in. deep-dish pie plate, layer first six ingredients; top with olives, if desired, and pepperoncini. Sprinkle with feta cheese. Refrigerate until serving. Serve with pita chips.

¼ CUP: 60 cal., 4g fat (1g sat. fat), 5mg chol., 210mg sod., 4g carb. (1g sugars, 1g fiber), 3g pro. *Diabetic exchanges:* ½ starch, ½ fat.

✱
DID YOU KNOW?

Salty, crumbly Greek feta cheese is traditionally made with sheep's or goat's milk, but most American brands are made with cow's milk instead.

Ⓠ CRANBERRY COCKTAIL

I adore the combination of flavors in this recipe. The secret is to thaw the lemonade so it's still slightly icy—this way the cocktail will be cool and refreshing. For a no-alcohol option, use peach juice and lemon-lime soda instead of schnapps and vodka.
—*Julie Danler, Bel Aire, KS*

TAKES: 10 min. • **MAKES:** 4 servings

Ice cubes
4 oz. vodka
4 oz. peach schnapps liqueur
4 oz. thawed lemonade concentrate
4 oz. cranberry-raspberry juice
16 maraschino cherries

1. Fill a shaker three-fourths full with ice cubes.

2. Add vodka, schnapps, lemonade concentrate and juice to shaker; cover and shake for 10-15 seconds or until condensation forms on outside of shaker. Strain into four cocktail glasses. Place a skewer with four cherries in each glass.

1 SERVING: 226 cal., 0 fat (0 sat. fat), 0 chol., 4mg sod., 33g carb. (31g sugars, 0 fiber), 0 pro.

ITALIAN MEATBALL BUNS

These soft little rolls come with a surprise inside—savory Italian meatballs. They're wonderful dipped in marinara sauce, making them fun for my grandkids and for adults, too. I love how easy they are to put together.
—*Trina Linder-Mobley, Clover, SC*

PREP: 30 min. + rising • **BAKE:** 15 min. • **MAKES:** 2 dozen

12 frozen bread dough dinner rolls
1 pkg. (12 oz.) frozen fully cooked Italian meatballs, thawed
2 Tbsp. olive oil
¼ cup grated Parmesan cheese
¼ cup minced fresh basil
1½ cups marinara sauce, warmed

1. Let bread dough stand at room temperature for 25-30 minutes or until softened.

2. Cut each roll in half. Wrap each portion around a meatball, enclosing meatball completely; pinch dough firmly to seal. Place on greased baking sheets, seam side down. Cover with kitchen towels; let rise in a warm place until almost doubled, about 1½-2 hours.

3. Preheat oven to 350°. Bake buns 12-15 minutes or until golden brown. Brush tops with oil; sprinkle with cheese and basil. Serve with marinara sauce.

1 BUN WITH 1 TBSP. SAUCE: 112 cal., 5g fat (2g sat. fat), 8mg chol., 248mg sod., 12g carb. (2g sugars, 1g fiber), 5g pro.

BAKED ONION DIP

Some people like this cheesy dip so much that they can't tear themselves away from the appetizer table to eat their dinner.
—*Mona Zignego, Hartford, WI*

PREP: 5 min. • **BAKE:** 40 min. • **MAKES:** 2 cups

1 cup mayonnaise
1 cup chopped sweet onion
1 Tbsp. grated Parmesan cheese
¼ tsp. garlic salt
1 cup shredded Swiss cheese
Minced fresh parsley, optional
Assorted crackers

1. In a large bowl, combine mayonnaise, onion, Parmesan cheese and garlic salt; stir in Swiss cheese. Spoon into a 1-qt. baking dish.

2. Bake, uncovered, at 325° for 40 minutes or until golden brown. If desired, sprinkle with parsley. Serve with crackers.

2 TBSP.: 131 cal., 13g fat (3g sat. fat), 11mg chol., 127mg sod., 1g carb. (1g sugars, 0 fiber), 2g pro.

EASY TORTELLINI
SPINACH SOUP, 87

CHAPTER 3

SHORTCUT SOUPS & BREADS

Nothing beats the old-fashioned goodness of aromatic, fresh-baked bread and a steaming bowl of nourishing soup. These come together quickly with heartwarming rewards.

ⓠ ROSEMARY CHEDDAR MUFFINS

My stepmother gave me this recipe nearly 30 years ago. We have enjoyed these luscious biscuitlike muffins ever since. You might not even need butter!
—*Bonnie Stallings, Martinsburg, WV*

TAKES: 25 min. • **MAKES:** 1 dozen

2 cups self-rising flour
½ cup shredded sharp cheddar cheese
1 Tbsp. minced fresh rosemary or 1 tsp. dried rosemary, crushed
1¼ cups 2% milk
3 Tbsp. mayonnaise

1. Preheat oven to 400°. In a large bowl, combine flour, cheese and rosemary. In another bowl, combine milk and mayonnaise; stir into dry ingredients just until moistened. Spoon into 12 greased muffin cups.

2. Bake 8-10 minutes or until lightly browned and toothpick inserted in muffin comes out clean. Cool 5 minutes before removing from pan to a wire rack. Serve warm.

NOTE: To substitute each cup of self-rising flour, place 1½ tsp. baking powder and ½ tsp. salt in a measuring cup. Add all-purpose flour to measure 1 cup.

1 MUFFIN: 121 cal., 5g fat (2g sat. fat), 8mg chol., 300mg sod., 16g carb. (1g sugars, 0 fiber), 4g pro.

ⓢ SALMON SWEET POTATO SOUP

I created this recipe as a healthier alternative to whitefish chowder, which is a favorite in the area where I grew up. Salmon and sweet potatoes boost the nutrition, and the slow cooker makes this soup convenient. It's especially comforting on a cold fall or winter day!
—*Matthew Hass, Franklin, WI*

PREP: 20 min. • **COOK:** 5½ hours • **MAKES:** 8 servings (3 qt.)

1 Tbsp. olive oil
1 medium onion, chopped
1 medium carrot, chopped
1 celery rib, chopped
3 garlic cloves, minced
2 medium sweet potatoes, peeled and cut into ½-in. cubes
1½ cups frozen corn, thawed
6 cups reduced-sodium chicken broth
1 tsp. celery salt
1 tsp. dill weed
½ tsp. salt
¾ tsp. pepper
1½ lbs. salmon fillets, skin removed, cut into ¾-in. pieces
1 can (12 oz.) fat-free evaporated milk
2 Tbsp. minced fresh parsley

1. In a large skillet, heat oil over medium heat. Add onion, carrot and celery; cook and stir until tender, 4-5 minutes. Add garlic; cook 1 minute longer. Transfer to a 5-qt. slow cooker. Add the next seven ingredients. Cook, covered, on low until sweet potatoes are tender, 5-6 hours.

2. Stir in salmon, milk and parsley. Cook, covered, until the fish just begins to flake easily with a fork, 30-40 minutes longer.

1½ CUPS: 279 cal., 10g fat (2g sat. fat), 45mg chol., 834mg sod., 26g carb. (13g sugars, 3g fiber), 22g pro. *Diabetic exchanges:* 3 lean meat, 1½ starch, ½ fat.

ⓠ MUSHROOM CHEESE BREAD

This savory grilled bread is delightful with barbecued steak, baked potatoes and corn on the cob. For a variation, we sometimes use half cheddar cheese and half mozzarella.
—*Dolly McDonald, Edmonton, AB*

TAKES: 15 min. • **MAKES:** 12 servings

1 cup shredded part-skim mozzarella cheese
1 can (4 oz.) mushroom stems and pieces, drained
⅓ cup mayonnaise
2 Tbsp. shredded Parmesan cheese
2 Tbsp. chopped green onion
1 loaf (1 lb.) unsliced French bread

1. In a small bowl, combine the mozzarella cheese, mushrooms, mayonnaise, Parmesan cheese and onion. Cut bread in half lengthwise; spread cheese mixture over cut sides.

2. Grill, covered, over indirect heat or broil 4 in. from the heat for 5-10 minutes or until lightly browned. Slice and serve warm.

1 SERVING: 180 cal., 8g fat (2g sat. fat), 10mg chol., 347mg sod., 20g carb. (1g sugars, 1g fiber), 6g pro.

ⓠ EASY TORTELLINI SPINACH SOUP

This is the easiest soup you will ever make—take it from me! I always keep the ingredients on hand so if I'm feeling under the weather or just plain busy, I can throw together this comforting soup in a flash.
—*Angela Lively, Conroe, TX*

TAKES: 20 min. • **MAKES:** 8 servings (3 qt.)

16 frozen fully cooked Italian meatballs (about 1 lb.)
1 can (14½ oz.) fire-roasted diced tomatoes, undrained
¼ tsp. Italian seasoning
¼ tsp. pepper
2 cartons (32 oz. each) chicken stock
2 cups frozen cheese tortellini (about 8 oz.)
3 oz. fresh baby spinach (about 4 cups)
Shredded Parmesan cheese, optional

1. Place first five ingredients in a 6-qt. stockpot; bring to a boil. Reduce heat; simmer, covered, 10 minutes.

2. Return to a boil. Add tortellini; cook, uncovered, until meatballs are heated through and tortellini are tender, 3-5 minutes, stirring occasionally. Stir in spinach until wilted. Serve immediately. If desired, top with Parmesan cheese.

1½ CUPS: 177 cal., 8g fat (4g sat. fat), 18mg chol., 949mg sod., 14g carb. (3g sugars, 1g fiber), 12g pro.

TEST KITCHEN TIP

Fully cooked Italian sausage, cut into half-moon slices, may be substituted for the meatballs. One 9-oz. package of refrigerated cheese tortellini may be substituted for 2 cups frozen tortellini.

🅢 NAVY BEAN VEGETABLE SOUP

My family really likes bean soup, so I came up with this enticing version. The leftovers are, dare I say, even better the next day!
—*Eleanor Mielke, Mitchell, SD*

PREP: 15 min. • **COOK:** 9 hours • **MAKES:** 12 servings (3 qt.)

4 medium carrots, thinly sliced
2 celery ribs, chopped
1 medium onion, chopped
2 cups cubed fully cooked ham
1½ cups dried navy beans
1 envelope vegetable recipe mix (Knorr)
1 envelope onion soup mix
1 bay leaf
½ tsp. pepper
8 cups water

In a 5-qt. slow cooker, combine the first nine ingredients. Stir in water. Cover and cook on low for 9-10 hours or until beans are tender. Discard bay leaf.

1 CUP: 157 cal., 2g fat (1g sat. fat), 12mg chol., 763mg sod., 24g carb. (4g sugars, 8g fiber), 11g pro.

TEST KITCHEN TIP

Beans pack a nutritional one-two punch of protein and fiber, which helps you feel fuller longer. They're an economical way to stretch the meat in soups and other dishes. And, nope, you don't have to soak the beans overnight in this recipe.

CHEESE-FILLED GARLIC ROLLS

To change up plain old dinner rolls, I added mozzarella. Now my family wants them at every gathering. I don't mind, even in a time crunch.
—*Rosalie Fittery, Philadelphia, PA*

PREP: 20 min. + rising • **BAKE:** 15 min. • **MAKES:** 2 dozen

1 loaf (1 lb.) frozen bread dough, thawed
24 cubes part-skim mozzarella cheese (¾ in. each, about 10 oz.)
3 Tbsp. butter, melted
2 tsp. minced fresh parsley
1 garlic clove, minced
½ tsp. Italian seasoning
½ tsp. crushed red pepper flakes
2 Tbsp. grated Parmigiano-Reggiano cheese

1. Divide dough into 24 portions. Shape each portion around a cheese cube to cover completely; pinch to seal. Place each roll in a greased muffin cup, seam side down. Cover with kitchen towels; let rise in a warm place until doubled, about 30 minutes. Preheat the oven to 350°.

2. In a small bowl, mix butter, parsley, garlic, Italian seasoning and pepper flakes. Brush over rolls; sprinkle with cheese. Bake until golden brown, 15-18 minutes.

3. Cool rolls for 5 minutes before removing from pans. Serve warm.

1 ROLL: 103 cal., 5g fat (2g sat. fat), 12mg chol., 205mg sod., 10g carb. (1g sugars, 1g fiber), 5g pro.

TURKEY SAUSAGE, BUTTERNUT & KALE SOUP

Kale and butternut squash are two of my favorite fall veggies.
This recipe combines them into a warm and comforting soup.
If you love sweet potatoes, sub them for the squash.
—*Laura Koch, Lincoln, NE*

PREP: 20 min. • **COOK:** 30 min. • **MAKES:** 10 servings (2½ qt.)

1 pkg. (19½ oz.) Italian turkey sausage links, casings removed
1 medium butternut squash (about 3 lbs.), peeled and cubed
2 cartons (32 oz. each) reduced-sodium chicken broth
1 bunch kale, trimmed and coarsely chopped (about 16 cups)
½ cup shaved Parmesan cheese

1. In a stockpot, cook sausage over medium heat for 8-10 minutes or until no longer pink, breaking the meat into crumbles.

2. Add squash and broth; bring to a boil. Gradually stir in kale, allowing it to wilt slightly between additions. Return to a boil. Reduce heat; simmer, uncovered, 15-20 minutes or until vegetables are tender. Top servings with cheese.

1 CUP: 163 cal., 5g fat (2g sat. fat), 23mg chol., 838mg sod., 20g carb. (5g sugars, 5g fiber), 13g pro.

KIDS' FAVORITE CHILI

This sweet and easy chili is sure to warm up the whole family on those chilly fall nights. The recipe has been in my family for three generations.
—*Terri Keeney, Greeley, CO*

TAKES: 25 min. • **MAKES:** 4 servings

1 lb. ground turkey
½ cup chopped onion
1 can (15¾ oz.) pork and beans
1 can (14½ oz.) diced tomatoes, undrained
1 can (10¾ oz.) condensed tomato soup, undiluted
1 Tbsp. brown sugar
1 Tbsp. chili powder

In a large saucepan, cook turkey and onion over medium heat until meat is no longer pink; drain. Stir in the remaining ingredients. Bring to a boil. Reduce heat; cover and simmer for 15-20 minutes or until heated through.

1½ CUPS: 359 cal., 10g fat (2g sat. fat), 75mg chol., 908mg sod., 43g carb. (20g sugars, 9g fiber), 30g pro.

DID YOU KNOW?

This simple chili is a little high in sodium. If you switch to no-salt-added diced tomatoes and reduced-sodium condensed soup, you can bring the sodium down by 30 percent—to 634mg per serving.

① CHEDDAR CORN DOG MUFFINS

I wanted a change from hot dogs, so I made corn dog muffins. I added jalapenos to this kid-friendly recipe and that won my husband over, too.
—*Becky Tarala, Palm Coast, FL*

TAKES: 25 min. • **MAKES:** 9 muffins

1 pkg. (8½ oz.) cornbread/ muffin mix
⅔ cup 2% milk
1 large egg, lightly beaten
5 turkey hot dogs, sliced
½ cup shredded sharp cheddar cheese
2 Tbsp. finely chopped pickled jalapeno, optional

1. Preheat oven to 400°. Line nine muffin cups with foil liners or grease nine nonstick muffin cups.

2. In a small bowl, combine muffin mix, milk and egg; stir in hot dogs, cheese and, if desired, jalapeno. Fill prepared cups three-fourths full.

3. Bake 14-18 minutes or until a toothpick inserted in center comes out clean. Cool 5 minutes before removing from the pan to a wire rack. Serve warm. Refrigerate leftovers.

FREEZE OPTION: Freeze cooled muffins in resealable plastic freezer bags. To use, microwave each muffin on high for 30-60 seconds or until heated through.

1 MUFFIN: 216 cal., 10g fat (4g sat. fat), 46mg chol., 619mg sod., 23g carb. (7g sugars, 2g fiber), 8g pro.

ITALIAN MEATBALL-BEAN SOUP

In North Dakota, it's pretty common for winter temps
to fall below zero. Hearty soups like this are a must.
—*Noelle Myers, Grand Forks, ND*

PREP: 35 min. • **COOK:** 15 min. • **MAKES:** 8 servings (3 qt.)

1 large egg, lightly beaten
½ cup savory herb or chicken stuffing mix, crushed
¼ tsp. salt
1 lb. ground chicken

SOUP
1 Tbsp. olive oil
3 celery ribs, chopped
2 medium carrots, chopped
1 small onion, chopped
2 tsp. Italian seasoning
2 garlic cloves, minced
3 cans (15 oz. each) cannellini beans, rinsed and drained
6 cups reduced-sodium chicken broth
1½ tsp. grated lemon zest
5 oz. fresh baby spinach (about 6 cups)
2 Tbsp. lemon juice

1. Preheat oven to 400°. In a large bowl, combine egg, stuffing mix and salt. Add the chicken; mix lightly but thoroughly. Shape into 1¼-in. balls. Place in a greased 15x10x1-in. baking pan. Bake 14-17 minutes or until cooked through.

2. Meanwhile, in a 6-qt. stockpot, heat oil over medium heat. Add celery, carrots and onion; cook and stir for 5-7 minutes or until carrots are softened. Stir in Italian seasoning and garlic; cook 1 minute longer.

3. Add beans, broth and lemon zest; bring to a boil. Reduce heat to low. Stir in spinach and meatballs; cook just until spinach is wilted. Stir in lemon juice.

1½ CUPS: 265 cal., 8g fat (2g sat. fat), 61mg chol., 828mg sod., 30g carb. (2g sugars, 8g fiber), 20g pro.

CHICKEN, ASPARAGUS & CORN CHOWDER

Chicken and asparagus make a light, comforting soup that's easy to put together with common ingredients. If we have rotisserie chicken, it goes into this soup.
—*Jennifer Vo, Irvine, CA*

TAKES: 30 min. • **MAKES:** 4 servings

2 Tbsp. olive oil
¾ cup cut fresh asparagus (1-in. pieces)
1 small onion, finely chopped
2 Tbsp. all-purpose flour
½ tsp. salt
¼ tsp. garlic powder
⅛ to ¼ tsp. pepper
1 can (14½ oz.) chicken broth
½ cup fat-free half-and-half cream
1½ cups cubed cooked chicken breast
¾ cup frozen corn

1. In a large saucepan, heat oil over medium heat. Add asparagus and onion; cook and stir for 3-4 minutes or until tender.

2. Stir in the flour, salt, garlic powder and pepper until blended; gradually stir in broth and half-and-half. Bring to a boil, stirring constantly; cook and stir 3-5 minutes or until slightly thickened. Add the chicken and corn; heat through.

1 CUP: 215 cal., 9g fat (1g sat. fat), 43mg chol., 800mg sod., 15g carb. (4g sugars, 1g fiber), 19g pro.

PESTO PULL-APART BREAD

I combined some of my favorite flavors to create an easy bread to complement our Italian meal. I make homemade pesto, oven-dried tomatoes and roasted red peppers, but store-bought will work just as well.
—*Sue Gronholz, Beaver Dam, WI*

PREP: 10 min. • **BAKE:** 30 min. • **MAKES:** 1 loaf (16 servings)

1 tube (16.3 oz.) large refrigerated buttermilk biscuits
¼ cup olive oil
2 Tbsp. prepared pesto
¼ cup sun-dried tomatoes (not packed in oil)
¼ cup roasted sweet red peppers, drained and diced
¼ cup sliced ripe olives
1 cup shredded mozzarella and provolone cheese blend
Additional prepared pesto, optional

1. Preheat oven to 350°. Cut each biscuit into 4 pieces. Combine olive oil and pesto. Dip biscuit pieces into pesto mixture until coated; place in an 8-in. round baking pan. Top with sun-dried tomatoes, roasted red peppers and ripe olives.

2. Bake until golden brown, about 25 minutes. Sprinkle with cheese. Return to oven; bake until melted, 5 minutes longer. Cut into wedges or pull apart; serve warm with additional pesto if desired.

1 SERVING: 152 cal., 9g fat (3g sat. fat), 5mg chol., 410mg sod., 13g carb. (2g sugars, 1g fiber), 3g pro.

TEST KITCHEN TIP

Serve this bread with dinner, as an appetizer or even for brunch. You can't go wrong. Want more cheese? Serve some warm cheese dip on the side for dunking.

SC SLOW-COOKED MEXICAN BEEF SOUP

My family loves this stew, and I'm happy to make it since it's so simple! You can serve it with cornbread instead of chips to make it an even more filling meal.
—*Angela Lively, Conroe, TX*

PREP: 15 min. • **COOK:** 6 hours • **MAKES:** 6 servings (2 qt.)

1 lb. beef stew meat (1¼-in. pieces)

¾ lb. potatoes (about 2 medium), cut into ¾-in. cubes

2 cups frozen corn (about 10 oz.), thawed

2 medium carrots, cut into ½-in. slices

1 medium onion, chopped

2 garlic cloves, minced

1½ tsp. dried oregano

1 tsp. ground cumin

½ tsp. salt

¼ tsp. crushed red pepper flakes

2 cups beef stock

1 can (10 oz.) diced tomatoes and green chilies, undrained

Sour cream and tortilla chips, optional

In a 5- or 6-qt. slow cooker, combine the first 12 ingredients. Cook, covered, on low until meat is tender, 6-8 hours. If desired, serve with sour cream and chips.

1⅓ CUPS: 218 cal., 6g fat (2g sat. fat), 47mg chol., 602mg sod., 24g carb. (5g sugars, 3g fiber), 19g pro. *Diabetic exchanges:* 2 lean meat, 1½ starch.

ⓠ QUICK CHICKEN & WILD RICE SOUP

My mother-in-law raves about the chicken and rice soup we serve
at our house. I tweaked the recipe several times to get it just right.
—*Teresa Jacobson, St. Johns, FL*

TAKES: 30 min. • **MAKES:** 4 servings

1 pkg. (6.2 oz.) fast-
  cooking long grain and
  wild rice mix
2 Tbsp. butter
1 small onion, finely
  chopped
1 celery rib, finely chopped
1 medium carrot, finely
  chopped
1 garlic clove, minced
2 Tbsp. all-purpose flour
3 cups 2% milk
1½ cups chicken broth
2 cups cubed cooked
  chicken

1. Cook rice mix according to package directions.

2. Meanwhile, in a large saucepan, heat butter over medium-high heat. Add onion, celery and carrot; cook and stir 6-8 minutes or until tender. Add garlic; cook 1 minute longer. Stir in flour until blended; gradually whisk in milk and chicken broth. Bring to a boil, stirring constantly; cook and stir 1-2 minutes longer or until slightly thickened.

3. Stir in chicken and rice; heat through.

2 CUPS: 465 cal., 15g fat (7g sat. fat), 94mg chol., 1095mg sod., 50g carb. (12g sugars, 2g fiber), 32g pro.

S'MORES MONKEY BREAD MUFFINS

When it comes to mini versions of anything, I'm sold! These are single-sized monkey breads made with frozen dinner rolls, graham cracker crumbs, chocolate chips and mini marshmallows. They couldn't be easier to make, and kids just love them.
—Tina Butler, Royse City, TX

PREP: 35 min. • **BAKE:** 15 min. • **MAKES:** 1 dozen

15 frozen bread dough dinner rolls, thawed but still cold
1⅓ cups graham cracker crumbs
½ cup sugar
6 Tbsp. butter, cubed
1 cup miniature semisweet chocolate chips, divided
¾ cup miniature marshmallows
ICING
1 cup confectioners' sugar
½ tsp. butter, softened
1 to 2 Tbsp. 2% milk

1. Preheat oven to 375°. Line 12 muffin cups with foil liners.

2. Using a sharp knife, cut each dinner roll into four pieces. In a shallow bowl, mix cracker crumbs and sugar. In a large microwave-safe bowl, microwave butter until melted. Dip three pieces of dough in butter, then roll in crumb mixture to coat; place in a prepared muffin cup. Repeat until all muffin cups are filled. Sprinkle tops with ¾ cup chocolate chips and marshmallows.

3. Toss remaining dough pieces with remaining butter, rewarming butter if necessary. Place two additional dough pieces into each cup; sprinkle with remaining chocolate chips.

4. Bake until golden brown, 15-20 minutes. Cool for 5 minutes before removing from pan to a wire rack. Mix icing ingredients; spoon over tops. Serve warm.

1 MUFFIN: 351 cal., 13g fat (6g sat. fat), 16mg chol., 337mg sod., 57g carb. (29g sugars, 3g fiber), 6g pro.

🅢 CREAM OF POTATO & CHEDDAR SOUP

The Yukon Gold potatoes my daughter shares from her garden make this soup incredible. Add some cheddar cheese and crisp croutons, and it's just heavenly. Total comfort with the simplicity of good ingredients!
—*Cindi Bauer, Marshfield, WI*

PREP: 25 min. • **COOK:** 7½ hours • **MAKES:** 11 servings (2¾ qt.)

8 medium Yukon Gold potatoes, peeled and cubed
1 large red onion, chopped
1 celery rib, chopped
2 cans (14½ oz. each) reduced-sodium chicken broth
1 can (10¾ oz.) condensed cream of celery soup, undiluted
1 tsp. garlic powder
½ tsp. white pepper
1½ cups shredded sharp cheddar cheese
1 cup half-and-half cream
Optional toppings: salad croutons, crumbled cooked bacon and additional shredded sharp cheddar cheese

1. Combine the first seven ingredients in a 4- or 5-qt. slow cooker. Cover and cook on low for 7-9 hours or until potatoes are tender.

2. Stir in cheese and cream. Cover and cook 30 minutes longer or until cheese is melted. Garnish servings with toppings of your choice.

1 CUP: 212 cal., 8g fat (5g sat. fat), 28mg chol., 475mg sod., 27g carb. (4g sugars, 3g fiber), 8g pro. *Diabetic exchanges:* 2 starch, 1½ fat.

DID YOU KNOW?
White pepper comes from fully ripened peppercorns that have had their skins removed. It has a milder flavor than black pepper and is helpful in dishes like mashed potatoes where you might not want black flecks to show. You can substitute black pepper (perhaps using a bit less than called for).

ⓠ MUSHROOM TORTELLINI SOUP

This nutritious veggie soup eats like a meal thanks to cheese tortellini. It's a real comfort on a cold or rainy day.
—*Jen Lucas, Baldwinville, MA*

TAKES: 25 min. • **MAKES:** 6 servings

2 Tbsp. olive oil
½ lb. sliced fresh mushrooms
2 garlic cloves, minced
4 cups vegetable broth
1 can (14½ oz.) diced tomatoes with basil, oregano and garlic, undrained
1 pkg. (19 oz.) frozen cheese tortellini
2 cups fresh baby spinach, coarsely chopped
⅛ tsp. pepper
Shredded Parmesan cheese, optional

1. In a Dutch oven, heat oil over medium-high heat. Add mushrooms; cook and stir 6-8 minutes or until tender. Add garlic; cook 1 minute longer.

2. Add broth and tomatoes; bring to a boil. Add tortellini; cook, uncovered, 3-4 minutes or just until tortellini float (do not boil). Stir in spinach and pepper; cook just until spinach is wilted. If desired, serve with shredded Parmesan.

1⅓ CUPS: 261 cal., 10g fat (3g sat. fat), 14mg chol., 1084mg sod., 32g carb. (5g sugars, 3g fiber), 10g pro.

SWISS & CARAWAY FLATBREADS

My mom came across this rustic-looking flatbread many years ago and always made it on Christmas Eve. Now I make it for my own family throughout the year. It's easy to cut the recipe in half if you're serving fewer people.
—*Diane Berger, Sequim, WA*

PREP: 20 min. + rising • **BAKE:** 10 min. • **MAKES:** 2 loaves (16 pieces each)

- 2 loaves (1 lb. each) frozen bread dough, thawed
- ¼ cup butter, melted
- ¼ cup canola oil
- 1 Tbsp. dried minced onion
- 1 Tbsp. Dijon mustard
- 2 tsp. caraway seeds
- 1 tsp. Worcestershire sauce
- 1 Tbsp. dry sherry, optional
- 2 cups shredded Swiss cheese

1. On a lightly floured surface, roll each portion of dough into a 15x10-in. rectangle. Transfer to two greased 15x10x1-in. baking pans. Cover with kitchen towels; let rise in a warm place until doubled, about 45 minutes.

2. Preheat oven to 425°. Using fingertips, press several dimples into dough. In a small bowl, whisk butter, oil, onion, mustard, caraway seeds, Worcestershire sauce and, if desired, sherry until blended; brush over dough. Sprinkle with cheese. Bake 10-15 minutes or until golden brown. Serve warm.

FREEZE OPTION: Cut cooled flatbreads into pieces. Freeze in resealable plastic freezer bags. To use, reheat flatbreads on an ungreased baking sheet in a preheated 425° oven until heated through.

1 PIECE: 134 cal., 6g fat (2g sat. fat), 10mg chol., 199mg sod., 14g carb. (1g sugars, 1g fiber), 5g pro.

ⓠ SHRIMP EGG DROP SOUP

Who knew egg drop soup was so easy? It's just three simple steps to make this better-than-restaurant-quality soup with just the right blend of veggies and shrimp.
— *Taste of Home* Test Kitchen

. . . .

TAKES: 30 min. • **MAKES:** 4 servings

4 tsp. cornstarch
½ tsp. soy sauce
⅛ tsp. ground ginger
1½ cups cold water, divided
2 cans (14½ oz. each) chicken broth
1½ cups frozen home-style egg noodles
1 cup frozen broccoli florets, thawed and coarsely chopped
½ cup julienned carrot
1 large egg, lightly beaten
½ lb. cooked medium shrimp, peeled and deveined

1. In a small bowl, combine the cornstarch, soy sauce, ginger and ½ cup cold water; set aside.

2. In a large saucepan, combine chicken broth and remaining water. Bring to a simmer; add noodles. Cook, uncovered, for 15 minutes. Add broccoli and carrot; simmer 3-4 minutes longer or until the noodles are tender.

3. Drizzle beaten egg into hot soup, stirring constantly. Stir cornstarch mixture and add to the pan. Bring to a boil; cook and stir 2 minutes or until slightly thickened. Add shrimp; heat through.

1¼ CUPS: 241 cal., 4g fat (1g sat. fat), 196mg chol., 1050mg sod., 30g carb. (3g sugars, 2g fiber), 18g pro.

MACARONI COLESLAW, 147

CHAPTER 4

SALADS & SIDES

Here you'll find easy-prep salads and side dishes for all occasions, from traditional holiday casseroles to fruity, fanciful picnic salads.

....

ⓈⒸ CORN & BROCCOLI IN CHEESE SAUCE

This veggie side dish is a standby. My daughter likes to add leftover ham to it. Save room in the oven by making it in your slow cooker.
—*Joyce Johnson, Uniontown, OH*

PREP: 10 min. • **COOK:** 3 hours • **MAKES:** 8 servings

1 pkg. (16 oz.) frozen corn, thawed

1 pkg. (16 oz.) frozen broccoli florets, thawed

4 oz. reduced-fat process cheese (Velveeta), cubed

½ cup shredded cheddar cheese

1 can (10¼ oz.) reduced-fat reduced-sodium condensed cream of chicken soup, undiluted

¼ cup fat-free milk

1. In a 4-qt. slow cooker, combine the corn, broccoli and cheeses. In a small bowl, combine soup and milk; pour over vegetable mixture.

2. Cover and cook on low for 3-4 hours or until heated through. Stir before serving.

¾ CUP: 148 cal., 5g fat (3g sat. fat), 16mg chol., 409mg sod., 21g carb. (4g sugars, 3g fiber), 8g pro. *Diabetic exchanges:* 1 starch, 1 medium-fat meat.

ⓠ BACON-TOMATO SALAD

We love this wonderful salad that tastes like a piled-high BLT without the time, effort or carbs. Plus, you can make it hours ahead and keep it in the fridge until serving time.
—*Denise Thurman, Columbia, MO*

TAKES: 15 min. • **MAKES:** 6 servings

1 pkg. (12 oz.) iceberg lettuce blend
2 cups grape tomatoes, halved
¾ cup coleslaw salad dressing
¾ cup shredded cheddar cheese
12 bacon strips, cooked and crumbled

In a large bowl, combine lettuce blend and tomatoes. Drizzle with dressing; sprinkle with cheese and bacon.

1¼ CUPS: 268 cal., 20g fat (6g sat. fat), 41mg chol., 621mg sod., 11g carb. (9g sugars, 1g fiber), 10g pro.

TEST KITCHEN TIP
Substitute Vidalia onion dressing for the coleslaw dressing for a slightly sweeter variation.

CREAMY CARROT CASSEROLE

My mom and I developed this recipe to see if there was a carrot dish that even people who don't care for carrots would enjoy. So far, I haven't met anyone who hasn't liked this casserole.
—*Laurie Heward, Fillmore, UT*

PREP: 15 min. • **BAKE:** 30 min. • **MAKES:** 8 servings

1½ lbs. carrots, sliced or 1 pkg. (20 oz.) frozen sliced carrots, thawed
1 cup mayonnaise
1 Tbsp. grated onion
1 Tbsp. prepared horseradish
¼ cup shredded cheddar cheese
2 Tbsp. crushed Ritz crackers

1. Preheat oven to 350°. Place 1 in. of water in a large saucepan; add carrots. Bring to a boil. Reduce heat; cover and simmer for 7-9 minutes or until crisp-tender. Drain, reserving ¼ cup cooking liquid. Transfer carrots to a 1½-qt. baking dish.

2. In a small bowl, combine the mayonnaise, onion, horseradish and reserved cooking liquid; spread evenly over carrots. Sprinkle with cheese; top with cracker crumbs. Bake, uncovered, for 30 minutes.

¾ CUP: 238 cal., 22g fat (4g sat. fat), 6mg chol., 241mg sod., 10g carb. (4g sugars, 2g fiber), 2g pro.

LAYERED CORNBREAD SALAD

When the garden comes in, we harvest the veggies and layer them with cornbread and sweet relish for this snappy salad. Everyone wants seconds.
—*Rebecca Clark, Warrior, AL*

PREP: 45 min. + chilling • **MAKES:** 14 servings

1 pkg. (8½ oz.) cornbread/muffin mix
1 cup mayonnaise
½ cup sweet pickle relish
2 cans (15 oz. each) pinto beans, rinsed and drained
4 medium tomatoes, chopped
1 medium green pepper, chopped
1 medium onion, chopped
10 bacon strips, cooked and crumbled

1. Preheat oven to 400°. Prepare cornbread batter according to package directions. Pour into a greased 8-in. square baking pan. Bake 15-20 minutes or until a toothpick inserted in center comes out clean. Cool completely in pan on a wire rack.

2. Coarsely crumble cornbread into a large bowl. In a small bowl, mix mayonnaise and relish.

3. In a 3-qt. trifle bowl or glass bowl, layer a third of the cornbread and half of each of the following: beans, tomatoes, pepper, onion, bacon and the mayonnaise mixture. Repeat layers. Top with remaining cornbread. Refrigerate, covered, 2-4 hours before serving.

¾ CUP: 299 cal., 18g fat (3g sat. fat), 26mg chol., 491mg sod., 27g carb. (9g sugars, 4g fiber), 7g pro.

GREEN PEA CASSEROLE

This has been my family's favorite vegetable casserole for 20 years now! The kids requested it again and again for Thanksgiving dinner.
—*Barbara Preneta, Unionville, CT*

PREP: 15 min. • **BAKE:** 20 min. • **MAKES:** 8 servings

5 cups frozen peas (about 20 oz.), thawed
1 celery rib, chopped
½ cup mayonnaise
⅓ cup chopped onion
¼ tsp. salt
¼ tsp. pepper
1 pkg. (6 oz.) stuffing mix

Preheat oven to 350°. Mix first six ingredients; transfer to a greased 11x7-in baking dish. Prepare stuffing mix according to package directions. Spread over pea mixture. Bake, uncovered, until lightly browned, 20-25 minutes.

⅔ CUP: 293 cal., 17g fat (5g sat. fat), 16mg chol., 581mg sod., 29g carb. (6g sugars, 5g fiber), 7g pro.

CREAMY BLUEBERRY GELATIN SALAD

Plump blueberries and a fluffy topping star in this pretty, refreshing salad.
My mom's blueberry salad was served at every holiday and celebration.
Now, my grandchildren look forward to sampling it at family gatherings.
—*Sharon Hoefert, Greendale, WI*

PREP: 30 min. + chilling • **MAKES:** 15 servings

2 pkg. (3 oz. each) grape gelatin
2 cups boiling water
1 can (21 oz.) blueberry pie filling
1 can (20 oz.) unsweetened crushed pineapple, undrained

TOPPING
1 pkg. (8 oz.) cream cheese, softened
1 cup sour cream
½ cup sugar
1 tsp. vanilla extract
½ cup chopped walnuts

1. In a large bowl, dissolve gelatin in boiling water. Cool for 10 minutes. Stir in pie filling and pineapple until blended. Transfer to a 13x9-in. dish. Cover and refrigerate until partially set, about 1 hour.

2. For topping, in a small bowl, combine the cream cheese, sour cream, sugar and vanilla. Carefully spread over gelatin; sprinkle with chopped walnuts. Cover and refrigerate until firm.

1 PIECE: 221 cal., 10g fat (5g sat. fat), 27mg chol., 76mg sod., 29g carb. (26g sugars, 1g fiber), 4g pro.

STRAWBERRY GELATIN SALAD: Prepare salad with strawberry gelatin and pie filling instead of grape and blueberry. Stir in 1¼ cups chilled lemon-lime soda instead of the pineapple. Top if desired.

CHERRY COLA SALAD: Prepare salad with cherry gelatin and pie filling instead of grape and blueberry. Substitute 20 oz. crushed pineapple (drained) for undrained pineapple and add ¾ cup chilled cola. Omit the topping.

ⓠ HOLIDAY BRUSSELS SPROUTS

Make Brussels sprouts extra special for the holidays with peas, celery and, of course, bacon. The recipe doubles easily if needed.
—*Jodie Beckman, Council Bluffs, IA*

TAKES: 25 min. • **MAKES:** 6 servings

1 pkg. (16 oz.) frozen Brussels sprouts
1 pkg. (10 oz.) frozen peas
2 Tbsp. butter
2 celery ribs, chopped
2 bacon strips, cooked and crumbled
2 Tbsp. minced fresh chives

1. Cook Brussels sprouts and peas according to package directions; drain.

2. In a large skillet, heat butter over medium-high heat. Add celery; cook and stir until crisp-tender. Add Brussels sprouts, peas, bacon and minced chives; toss to combine.

⅔ CUP: 115 cal., 5g fat (3g sat. fat), 12mg chol., 147mg sod., 13g carb. (3g sugars, 5g fiber), 6g pro. *Diabetic exchanges:* 2 vegetable, 1 fat.

ⓠ MINTY PINEAPPLE FRUIT SALAD

Fresh mint adds bright flavor to this low-fat pineapple salad.
Give it a berry twist by using blueberries and raspberries in place of the
grapes, but don't forget the secret dressing ingredient—lemonade!
—*Janie Colle, Hutchinson, KS*

TAKES: 15 min. • **MAKES:** 8 servings

4 cups cubed fresh
pineapple

2 cups sliced fresh
strawberries

1 cup green grapes

3 Tbsp. thawed lemonade
concentrate

2 Tbsp. honey

1 Tbsp. minced fresh mint

Place fruit in a large bowl. In another bowl, mix the remaining ingredients; stir gently into fruit. Refrigerate, covered, until serving.

¾ CUP: 99 cal., 0 fat (0 sat. fat), 0 chol., 4mg sod., 26g carb. (21g sugars, 2g fiber), 1g pro. *Diabetic exchanges:* 1½ fruit, ½ starch.

DELUXE HASH BROWN CASSEROLE

My son-in-law gave me the recipe for this hash brown casserole,
which my kids say is addictive. It's also an amazing make-ahead dish.
—*Amy Oswalt, Burr, NE*

PREP: 10 min. • **BAKE:** 50 min. • **MAKES:** 12 servings

1½ cups sour cream onion dip
1 can (10¾ oz.) condensed cream of chicken soup, undiluted
1 envelope ranch salad dressing mix
1 tsp. onion powder
1 tsp. garlic powder
½ tsp. pepper
1 pkg. (30 oz.) frozen shredded hash brown potatoes, thawed
2 cups shredded cheddar cheese
½ cup crumbled cooked bacon

Preheat oven to 375°. In a large bowl, mix the first six ingredients; stir in the potatoes, cheese and bacon. Transfer to a greased 13x9-in. baking dish. Bake for 50-60 minutes or until golden brown.

FREEZE OPTION: Cover and freeze unbaked casserole. To use, partially thaw in refrigerator overnight. Remove from refrigerator 30 minutes before baking. Preheat the oven to 375°. Bake casserole as directed, increasing time to 1¼-1½ hours or until the top is golden brown and a thermometer inserted in the center reads 165°.

⅔ CUP: 273 cal., 17g fat (6g sat. fat), 36mg chol., 838mg sod., 20g carb. (2g sugars, 2g fiber), 10g pro.

ⓠ COLORFUL SPIRAL PASTA SALAD

The ingredients in this salad make a beautiful mix.
Better yet, you can set it out on the buffet and forget it,
as it will stay fresh for the duration of your party.
—*Amanda Cable, Boxford, MA*

TAKES: 20 min. • **MAKES:** 14 servings

1 pkg. (12 oz.) tricolor spiral pasta
4 cups fresh broccoli florets
1 pint grape tomatoes
1 can (6 oz.) pitted ripe olives, drained
⅛ tsp. salt
⅛ tsp. pepper
1½ cups Italian salad dressing with roasted red pepper and Parmesan

1. In a Dutch oven, cook pasta according to package directions, adding broccoli during the last 2 minutes of cooking. Drain and rinse in cold water.

2. Transfer to a large bowl. Add the tomatoes, olives, salt and pepper. Drizzle with salad dressing; toss to coat. Chill until serving.

¾ CUP: 149 cal., 4g fat (0 sat. fat), 0 chol., 513mg sod., 24g carb. (4g sugars, 2g fiber), 4g pro.

ⓠ MUSHROOM & PEA RICE PILAF

Anything can go into rice pilaf, so I add peas and baby portobello mushrooms for a springlike burst of color and a variety of textures.
—*Stacy Mullens, Gresham, OR*

TAKES: 25 min. • **MAKES:** 6 servings

1 pkg. (6.6 oz.) rice pilaf mix with toasted almonds
1 Tbsp. butter
1½ cups fresh or frozen peas
1 cup sliced baby portobello mushrooms

1. Prepare pilaf according to package directions.

2. In a large skillet, heat butter over medium heat. Add peas and mushrooms; cook and stir until tender, 6-8 minutes. Stir in rice.

⅔ CUP: 177 cal., 6g fat (2g sat. fat), 10mg chol., 352mg sod., 28g carb. (3g sugars, 3g fiber), 5g pro. *Diabetic exchanges:* 2 starch, ½ fat.

NECTARINE & BEET SALAD

Beets and nectarines sprinkled with feta cheese make a scrumptious new blend for a mixed green salad. The combination may seem unlikely, but I guarantee it will become a favorite.
—*Nicole Werner, Ann Arbor, MI*

TAKES: 10 min. • **MAKES:** 8 servings

2 pkg. (5 oz. each) spring mix salad greens
2 medium nectarines, sliced
½ cup balsamic vinaigrette
1 can (14½ oz.) sliced beets, drained
½ cup crumbled feta cheese

On a serving dish, toss greens and nectarines with balsamic vinaigrette. Top with beets and cheese; serve immediately.

1 CUP: 84 cal., 4g fat (1g sat. fat), 4mg chol., 371mg sod., 10g carb. (6g sugars, 3g fiber), 3g pro. *Diabetic exchanges:* 2 vegetable, ½ fat.

✳
TEST KITCHEN TIP

Torn fresh basil or mint make an excellent addition to this salad. Serve with buttermilk dressing instead of balsamic if desired.

ⓈⒸ OLD-FASHIONED SPOON BREAD

My spoon bread is moister than corn pudding made in the oven, and the cream cheese is a nice addition. It goes great with Thanksgiving turkey or Christmas ham.
—*Tamara Ellefson, Frederic, WI*

PREP: 15 min. • **COOK:** 3 hours • **MAKES:** 8 servings

1 pkg. (8 oz.) cream cheese, softened
⅓ cup sugar
1 cup 2% milk
2 large eggs
2 Tbsp. butter, melted
1 tsp. salt
¼ tsp. ground nutmeg
Dash pepper
2⅓ cups frozen corn, thawed
1 can (14¾ oz.) cream-style corn
1 pkg. (8½ oz.) cornbread/muffin mix

1. In a large bowl, beat cream cheese and sugar until smooth. Gradually beat in the milk. Beat in the eggs, butter, salt, nutmeg and pepper until blended. Stir in corn and cream-style corn. Stir in cornbread mix just until moistened.

2. Pour into a greased 3-qt. slow cooker. Cover and cook on high for 3-4 hours or until center is almost set.

½ CUP: 391 cal., 18g fat (10g sat. fat), 100mg chol., 832mg sod., 52g carb. (19g sugars, 2g fiber), 9g pro.

MACARONI COLESLAW

My friend Peggy brought this coleslaw to one of our picnics, and everyone liked it so much, we all had to have the recipe.
—*Sandra Matteson, Westhope, ND*

PREP: 25 min. + chilling • **MAKES:** 16 servings

1 pkg. (7 oz.) ring macaroni or ditalini
1 pkg. (14 oz.) coleslaw mix
2 medium onions, finely chopped
2 celery ribs, finely chopped
1 medium cucumber, finely chopped
1 medium green pepper, finely chopped
1 can (8 oz.) whole water chestnuts, drained and chopped

DRESSING
1½ cups Miracle Whip Light
⅓ cup sugar
¼ cup cider vinegar
½ tsp. salt
¼ tsp. pepper

1. Cook macaroni according to package directions; drain and rinse in cold water. Transfer to a large bowl; add the coleslaw mix, onions, celery, cucumber, green pepper and water chestnuts.

2. In a small bowl, whisk the dressing ingredients. Pour over salad; toss to coat. Cover and refrigerate for at least 1 hour.

¾ CUP: 150 cal., 5g fat (1g sat. fat), 6mg chol., 286mg sod., 24g carb. (12g sugars, 2g fiber), 3g pro. *Diabetic exchanges:* 1 starch, 1 vegetable, 1 fat.

DID YOU KNOW?

The term coleslaw is derived from the Dutch word *koolsla*, literally translated as cabbage salad. The term has evolved to refer to many types of crunchy, shredded vegetable salads that hold up well after being dressed.

ⓠ POUTINE

The ultimate in French-Canadian comfort food, poutine commonly features french fries topped with cheese curds and gravy. This side dish is quick to fix with frozen potatoes and a gravy mix, but it has all the traditional flavors you'd expect.
—*Shelisa Terry, Henderson, NV*

TAKES: 30 min. • **MAKES:** 4 servings

4 cups frozen french-fried potatoes
1 envelope brown gravy mix
¼ tsp. pepper
½ cup white cheddar cheese curds or cubed white cheddar cheese

1. Prepare fries according to package directions.

2. Meanwhile, prepare gravy mix according to package directions. Stir in pepper. Place fries on a serving plate; top with cheese curds and gravy.

1 SERVING: 244 cal., 13g fat (4g sat. fat), 17mg chol., 465mg sod., 26g carb. (2g sugars, 2g fiber), 7g pro.

Q FLUFFY GREEN GRAPE SALAD

I received this recipe from a cousin-in-law at a family reunion. Since then, I've brought it to many gatherings myself. We also like to eat it as a dessert.
—*Kelli Giffen, Barrie, ON*

TAKES: 20 min. • **MAKES:** 12 servings

2 cans (8 oz. each) crushed pineapple, undrained
1 pkg. (3.4 oz.) instant pistachio pudding mix
1 carton (12 oz.) frozen whipped topping, thawed
2 cups halved green grapes

In a large bowl, combine the pineapple and pudding mix; mix well. Cover and refrigerate for 10 minutes. Fold in the whipped topping and grapes. Refrigerate until serving.

½ CUP: 144 cal., 5g fat (5g sat. fat), 0 chol., 113mg sod., 23g carb. (17g sugars, 0 fiber), 0 pro.

CHEESY SUMMER SQUASH
FLATBREADS, 162

CHAPTER 5

EASY MEALS

Turn to these pages for quick, simple dinners
the whole family is sure to love.

ⓠ SKINNY COBB SALAD

This skinny version of Cobb salad has all the taste and creaminess with half the fat and calories. You can skip the coleslaw mix and use only lettuce, but I like the crunch you get with cabbage.
—Taylor Kiser, Brandon, FL

TAKES: 25 min. • **MAKES:** 4 servings

¼ cup fat-free plain Greek yogurt
2 Tbsp. reduced-fat ranch salad dressing
1 to 2 tsp. cold water

SALAD
3 cups coleslaw mix
3 cups chopped lettuce
1 large apple, chopped
½ cup crumbled reduced-fat feta or blue cheese
1 cup cubed cooked chicken breast
2 green onions, chopped
4 turkey bacon strips, chopped and cooked
1 can (15 oz.) garbanzo beans or chickpeas, rinsed and drained
1 small ripe avocado, peeled and cubed

1. Mix yogurt and dressing; thin with water as desired. Toss coleslaw mix with lettuce; divide greens among four plates.

2. Arrange remaining ingredients in rows over top or as desired. Drizzle with yogurt mixture.

1 SERVING: 324 cal., 13g fat (3g sat. fat), 48mg chol., 646mg sod., 31g carb. (11g sugars, 9g fiber), 23g pro. *Diabetic exchanges:* 2 lean meat, 2 fat, 1½ starch, 1 vegetable.

TEST KITCHEN TIP

Combining classic Cobb salad flavors with healthy ingredients—like Greek yogurt, chopped apple and garbanzo beans—makes this main-dish salad a win-win.

ⓢ GREEN CHILI CHOPS WITH SWEET POTATOES

It takes only a few minutes to combine the ingredients in a slow cooker,
and you'll have a satisfying, healthy dinner waiting for you at the end of the day.
We like to serve it with freshly baked garlic bread.
—*Marina Ashworth, Denver, CO*

PREP: 20 min. • **COOK:** 6 hours • **MAKES:** 4 servings

3 medium sweet potatoes, peeled and cut into ½-in. slices
1 large onion, chopped
1 large green pepper, coarsely chopped
1½ cups frozen corn
½ tsp. salt
¼ tsp. pepper
4 boneless pork loin chops (6 oz. each)
1 can (10 oz.) mild green enchilada sauce
½ cup sour cream
2 Tbsp. reduced-sodium teriyaki sauce

1. In a 6-qt. slow cooker, combine sweet potatoes, onion, green pepper, corn, salt and pepper. Top with pork chops. In a small bowl, mix enchilada sauce, sour cream and teriyaki sauce; pour over meat.

2. Cook, covered, on low for 6-8 hours or until meat is tender.

1 SERVING: 495 cal., 17g fat (7g sat. fat), 102mg chol., 909mg sod., 45g carb. (16g sugars, 5g fiber), 39g pro.

SOUTHWESTERN FISH TACOS

These bright tacos take me on an instant trip to sunny Southern California.
This recipe has been on my family's most-requested list for years.
—*Joan Hallford, North Richland Hills, TX*

TAKES: 20 min. • **MAKES:** 2 servings

¼ cup mayonnaise

¼ cup sour cream

2 Tbsp. minced fresh cilantro

4 tsp. taco seasoning, divided

½ lb. cod or haddock fillets, cut into 1-in. pieces

1 Tbsp. lemon juice

1 Tbsp. canola oil

4 taco shells

Optional ingredients: shredded lettuce, chopped tomato and lime wedges

1. For sauce, mix mayonnaise, sour cream, cilantro and 2 tsp. taco seasoning. In another bowl, toss cod with lemon juice and remaining taco seasoning.

2. In a skillet, heat oil over medium-high heat; saute cod just until it just begins to flake easily with a fork, 4-6 minutes (fish may break apart as it cooks). Spoon into taco shells; serve with sauce and remaining ingredients as desired.

2 TACOS: 506 cal., 38g fat (8g sat. fat), 52mg chol., 852mg sod., 20g carb. (1g sugars, 1g fiber), 20g pro.

TEST KITCHEN TIP

A simple switch to reduced-fat mayo and sour cream in the sauce will save more than 100 calories and 10g fat per serving.

CHICKEN ZUCCHINI CASSEROLE

A co-worker shared this recipe that was originally her grandmother's. When I make it, I use pre-cooked chicken from the grocery store and fresh zucchini my neighbor gives me from his garden.
—*Bev Dutro, Dayton, OH*

....

PREP: 20 min. • **BAKE:** 45 min. • **MAKES:** 6 servings

1 pkg. (6 oz.) stuffing mix
¾ cup butter, melted
3 cups diced zucchini
2 cups cubed cooked chicken breast
1 can (10¾ oz.) condensed cream of chicken soup, undiluted
1 medium carrot, shredded
½ cup chopped onion
½ cup sour cream

1. In a large bowl, combine stuffing mix and butter. Set aside ½ cup for topping. Add the zucchini, chicken, soup, carrot, onion and sour cream to the remaining stuffing mixture.

2. Transfer to a greased 11x7-in. baking dish. Sprinkle with reserved stuffing mixture. Bake, uncovered, at 350° for 40-45 minutes or until casserole is golden brown and bubbly.

1 CUP: 481 cal., 31g fat (18g sat. fat), 115mg chol., 1174mg sod., 27g carb. (6g sugars, 2g fiber), 21g pro.

CHEESY SUMMER SQUASH FLATBREADS

When you want a meatless meal with Mediterranean style, these flatbreads smothered with hummus, squash and mozzarella deliver the goods.
—*Matthew Hass, Franklin, WI*

TAKES: 30 min. • **MAKES:** 4 servings

3 small yellow summer squash, sliced ¼ in. thick
1 Tbsp. olive oil
½ tsp. salt
2 cups fresh baby spinach, coarsely chopped
2 naan flatbreads
⅓ cup roasted red pepper hummus
1 carton (8 oz.) fresh mozzarella cheese pearls
Pepper

1. Preheat oven to 425°. Toss squash with oil and salt; spread evenly in a 15x10x1-in. baking pan. Roast for 8-10 minutes or until tender. Transfer to a bowl; stir in spinach.

2. Place naan on a baking sheet; spread with hummus. Top with squash mixture and cheese. Bake on a lower oven rack 4-6 minutes or just until cheese is melted. Sprinkle with pepper.

½ TOPPED FLATBREAD: 332 cal., 20g fat (9g sat. fat), 47mg chol., 737mg sod., 24g carb. (7g sugars, 3g fiber), 15g pro.

TURKEY SALSA BOWLS WITH TORTILLA WEDGES

Delicious and nutritious, this dish was a favorite of the kids in the junior chef classes I taught at church. The recipe encouraged creativity and healthy eating as students designed their own salsa bowls using whole grains, vegetables and lean protein.
—*Jean Gottfried, Upper Sandusky, OH*

PREP: 15 min. • **COOK:** 25 min. • **MAKES:** 8 servings

1   lb. lean ground turkey
½   cup chopped sweet pepper
¼   cup thinly sliced celery
2   green onions, chopped
1   jar (16 oz.) medium salsa
1   can (16 oz.) kidney beans, rinsed and drained
1   cup uncooked instant brown rice
1   cup water
4   whole wheat tortillas (8 in.)
1   Tbsp. canola oil
8   cups torn romaine (about 1 head)
     Optional toppings: chopped tomatoes, sliced ripe olives, cubed avocado, shredded cheddar cheese and chopped green onions

1. Preheat oven to 400°. In a large skillet, cook and crumble turkey with pepper, celery and green onions over medium-high heat until meat is no longer pink, 5-7 minutes. Stir in salsa, beans, rice and water; bring to a boil. Reduce heat; simmer, covered, until liquid is absorbed, about 15 minutes.

2. Brush both sides of tortillas with oil; cut each into eight wedges. Arrange in a single layer on a baking sheet. Bake until lightly browned, 8-10 minutes.

3. To serve, divide lettuce among eight bowls; top with turkey mixture. Serve with tortilla wedges and toppings as desired.

1 SERVING: 279 cal., 7g fat (1g sat. fat), 39mg chol., 423mg sod., 36g carb. (4g sugars, 6g fiber), 18g pro.
Diabetic exchanges: 2 starch, 2 lean meat, 1 vegetable.

ⓠ SPINACH FETA TURNOVERS

These quick and easy turnovers are a favorite for my wife,
who says they are delicious and melt in your mouth.
—*David Baruch, Weston, FL*

TAKES: 30 min. • **MAKES:** 4 servings

2 large eggs
1 pkg. (10 oz.) frozen leaf spinach, thawed, squeezed dry and chopped
¾ cup crumbled feta cheese
2 garlic cloves, minced
¼ tsp. pepper
1 tube (13.8 oz.) refrigerated pizza crust
  Refrigerated tzatziki sauce, optional

1. In a bowl, whisk eggs; set aside 1 Tbsp. Combine the spinach, feta cheese, garlic, pepper and remaining beaten eggs.

2. Unroll pizza dough; roll into a 12-in. square. Cut into four 3-in. squares. Top each square with about ⅓ cup spinach mixture. Fold into a triangle and pinch edges to seal. Cut slits in top; brush with reserved egg.

3. Place on a greased baking sheet. Bake at 425° for 10-12 minutes or until golden brown. If desired, serve with tzatziki sauce.

1 TURNOVER: 361 cal., 9g fat (4g sat. fat), 104mg chol., 936mg sod., 51g carb. (7g sugars, 4g fiber), 17g pro.

DID YOU KNOW?
Greek in origin, tzatziki sauce is a blend of yogurt, cucumber, garlic, and often lemon and dill. You can make your own version with plain yogurt or sour cream, plus whichever of these flavor components you like.

ⓠ ASPARAGUS NICOISE SALAD

I've used my Nicoise as an appetizer or main-dish salad, and it's a winner every time I put it on the table. Here's to a colorful, do-ahead sure thing.
—*Jan Meyer, St. Paul, MN*

TAKES: 20 min. • **MAKES:** 4 servings

1 lb. small red potatoes (about 10), halved

1 lb. fresh asparagus, trimmed and halved crosswise

3 pouches (2½ oz. each) albacore white tuna in water

½ cup pitted Greek olives, halved, optional

½ cup zesty Italian salad dressing

1. Place potatoes in a large saucepan; add water to cover by 2 in. Bring to a boil. Reduce heat; cook, uncovered, 10-12 minutes or until tender, adding asparagus during the last 2-4 minutes of cooking. Drain potatoes and asparagus; immediately drop into ice water.

2. To serve, drain potatoes and asparagus; pat dry and divide among four plates. Add tuna and, if desired, olives. Drizzle with dressing.

1 SERVING: 233 cal., 8g fat (0 sat. fat), 22mg chol., 583mg sod., 23g carb. (4g sugars, 3g fiber), 16g pro. *Diabetic exchanges:* 2 lean meat, 1½ starch, 1½ fat, 1 vegetable.

❶ GARLIC SALMON LINGUINE

This garlicky pasta is so nice to make on busy weeknights because I usually have everything I need already on hand. I serve mine with asparagus, rolls and fruit.
—*Theresa Hagan, Glendale, AZ*

TAKES: 20 min. • **MAKES:** 6 servings

1 pkg. (16 oz.) linguine
⅓ cup olive oil
3 garlic cloves, minced
1 can (14¾ oz.) salmon, drained, bones and skin removed
¾ cup chicken broth
¼ cup minced fresh parsley
½ tsp. salt
⅛ tsp. cayenne pepper

1. Cook linguine according to package directions; drain.

2. Meanwhile, in a large skillet, heat oil over medium heat. Add garlic; cook and stir until tender, about 1 minute (do not allow to brown). Stir in remaining ingredients; heat through. Add linguine; toss gently to combine.

1 SERVING: 489 cal., 19g fat (3g sat. fat), 31mg chol., 693mg sod., 56g carb. (3g sugars, 3g fiber), 25g pro.

TEST KITCHEN TIP

To keep parsley fresh for up to a month, trim the stems and place the bunch in a tumbler with an inch of water. Be sure no leaves are in the water. Tie a produce bag around the tumbler to trap humidity inside; store in the refrigerator. Each time you use the parsley, change the water and turn the produce bag inside out so any moisture that has built up inside the bag can escape.

ℚ DAD'S FAVORITE BARBECUE MEAT LOAVES

It may sound old-fashioned, but it warms my heart to serve dishes that make my family and friends happy. This recipe does just that, and then some.
—*Leta Winters, Johnson City, TN*

TAKES: 30 min. • **MAKES:** 4 servings

1 large egg, lightly beaten
½ cup stuffing mix, crushed
3 Tbsp. 2% milk
2 Tbsp. grated Parmesan cheese
1 Tbsp. plus ¼ cup barbecue sauce, divided
1 lb. ground beef

1. Preheat oven to 425°. In a large bowl, combine egg, stuffing mix, milk, cheese and 1 Tbsp. barbecue sauce. Add beef; mix lightly but thoroughly. Shape into four 4x2-in. loaves in a foil-lined 15x10x1-in. baking pan.

2. Bake 15-20 minutes or until a thermometer reads 160°. Spread with the remaining barbecue sauce before serving.

FREEZE OPTION: Individually wrap cooled meat loaves in plastic and foil; freeze. To use, partially thaw meat loaves in refrigerator overnight. Unwrap and reheat in a greased 15x10x1-in. baking pan in a preheated 350° oven until heated through and a thermometer inserted in center reads 165°. Top each with 1 Tbsp. barbecue sauce before serving.

1 MINI MEAT LOAF: 305 cal., 16g fat (6g sat. fat), 120mg chol., 449mg sod., 15g carb. (8g sugars, 1g fiber), 24g pro.

ⓠ CRUNCHY ASIAN CHICKEN SALAD

I love this crunchy, citrusy salad. Once I even made my husband drive the hour to the nearest Applebee's restaurant just so I could eat it! That's when I decided to come up with my own version that's a great stand-in for the original. I'm happy and my husband is, too!
—*Mandy Bird, Holbrook, ID*

TAKES: 25 min. • **MAKES:** 4 servings

4 frozen breaded chicken tenders (about 8 oz.)
⅓ cup mayonnaise
3 Tbsp. honey
2 Tbsp. rice vinegar
1½ tsp. Dijon mustard
¼ tsp. sesame oil
1 pkg. (10 oz.) hearts of romaine salad mix
1 pkg. (14 oz.) coleslaw mix
¼ cup crispy chow mein noodles
⅓ cup sliced almonds, toasted

1. Cook chicken tenders according to package directions. Meanwhile, whisk together mayonnaise, honey, vinegar, mustard and sesame oil.

2. To serve, place the romaine and coleslaw mixes in a large bowl; toss with dressing. Divide among four plates. Cut chicken into bite-sized pieces; place over salads. Sprinkle with noodles and almonds.

NOTE: To toast nuts, bake in a shallow pan in a 350° oven for 5-10 minutes or cook in a skillet over low heat until lightly browned, stirring occasionally.

1 SERVING: 419 cal., 25g fat (3g sat. fat), 11mg chol., 602mg sod., 42g carb. (20g sugars, 7g fiber), 12g pro.

❶ EASY MEATBALL STROGANOFF

This recipe has fed not only my own family, but many neighborhood kids! They come running when I make this supper. It's one of those things you throw together after work on a busy day because you just know it works.
—*Julie May, Hattiesburg, MS*

. . . .

TAKES: 30 min. • **MAKES:** 4 servings

- 3 cups uncooked egg noodles
- 1 Tbsp. olive oil
- 1 pkg. (12 oz.) frozen fully cooked Italian meatballs, thawed
- 1½ cups beef broth
- 1 tsp. dried parsley flakes
- ¾ tsp. dried basil
- ½ tsp. salt
- ½ tsp. dried oregano
- ¼ tsp. pepper
- 1 cup heavy whipping cream
- ¾ cup sour cream

1. Cook egg noodles according to package directions for al dente; drain.

2. Meanwhile, in a large skillet, heat oil over medium-high heat. Brown meatballs; remove from pan. Add broth, stirring to loosen browned bits from pan. Add seasonings. Bring to a boil; cook 5-7 minutes or until liquid is reduced to ½ cup.

3. Add meatballs, noodles and cream. Bring to a boil. Reduce heat; simmer, covered, 3-5 minutes or until slightly thickened. Stir in sour cream; heat through.

1 SERVING: 717 cal., 57g fat (30g sat. fat), 172mg chol., 1291mg sod., 31g carb. (5g sugars, 2g fiber), 20g pro.

ⓠ PESTO FISH WITH PINE NUTS

I love fish, and Italian flavors are my favorite. This is a tasty
way to get more healthy fish into your diet.
—*Valery Anderson, Sterling Heights, MI*

TAKES: 15 min. • **MAKES:** 4 servings

2 envelopes pesto sauce mix, divided
4 cod fillets (6 oz. each)
¼ cup olive oil
½ cup shredded Parmesan or Romano cheese
½ cup pine nuts, toasted

TEST KITCHEN TIP

Common olive oil works better for cooking at high heat than virgin or extra-virgin oil. Higher grades have wonderful flavor for cold foods, but they have a lower smoke point.

1. Prepare one envelope of pesto sauce mix according to package directions; set aside. Sprinkle fillets with remaining pesto mix, patting to help adhere.

2. In a large skillet, heat oil over medium heat. Add fillets; cook 4-5 minutes on each side or until fish just begins to flake easily with a fork. Remove from heat. Sprinkle with Parmesan cheese and pine nuts. Serve with pesto sauce.

NOTE: To toast nuts, bake in a shallow pan in a 350° oven for 5-10 minutes or cook in a skillet over low heat until lightly browned, stirring occasionally.

1 FILLET WITH SCANT 3 TBSP. PESTO SAUCE: 560 cal., 39g fat (5g sat. fat), 72mg chol., 1522mg sod., 17g carb. (7g sugars, 1g fiber), 35g pro.

PESTO CHICKEN WITH PINE NUTS: Substitute 4 boneless skinless chicken breasts (6 oz. each) for the cod. Cook for 6-8 minutes on each side or until a thermometer reads 170°.

CHICKEN CHILE RELLENO CASSEROLE

My husband likes Mexican food and casseroles, so I combined the two. This chicken with poblanos and chilies really hits the spot.
—*Erica Ingram, Lakewood, OH*

PREP: 20 min. • **BAKE:** 35 min. + standing • **MAKES:** 8 servings

2 Tbsp. butter
2 poblano peppers, seeded and coarsely chopped
1 small onion, finely chopped
2 Tbsp. all-purpose flour
1 tsp. ground cumin
1 tsp. smoked paprika
¼ tsp. salt
⅔ cup 2% milk
1 pkg. (8 oz.) cream cheese, cubed
2 cups shredded pepper jack cheese
2 cups coarsely shredded rotisserie chicken
1 can (4 oz.) chopped green chilies
2 pkg. (8½ oz. each) cornbread/muffin mix

1. Preheat oven to 350°. In a large skillet, heat butter over medium-high heat. Add peppers and onion; cook and stir 4-6 minutes or until peppers are tender.

2. Stir in flour and seasonings until blended; gradually stir in milk. Bring to a boil, stirring constantly; cook and stir until thickened, about 1 minute. Stir in the cream cheese until blended. Add the pepper jack, chicken and green chilies; heat through, stirring to combine. Transfer to a greased 11x7-in. baking dish.

3. Prepare cornbread batter according to package directions. Spread batter over chicken mixture. Bake, uncovered, 35-40 minutes or until golden brown and a toothpick inserted in topping comes out clean. Let stand 10 minutes before serving.

1 SERVING: 610 cal., 34g fat (16g sat. fat), 151mg chol., 987mg sod., 51g carb. (16g sugars, 5g fiber), 27g pro.

ITALIAN CRUMB-CRUSTED BEEF ROAST

Italian-style panko crumbs and seasoning give this roast beef a special touch. It's a nice, effortless weeknight meal, so you can put your energy into relaxing.
—*Maria Regakis, Saugus, MA*

PREP: 10 min. • **BAKE:** 1¾ hours + standing • **MAKES:** 8 servings

- 1 beef sirloin tip roast (3 lbs.)
- ¼ tsp. salt
- ¾ cup Italian-style panko (Japanese) bread crumbs
- ¼ cup mayonnaise
- 3 Tbsp. dried minced onion
- ½ tsp. Italian seasoning
- ¼ tsp. pepper

1. Preheat oven to 325°. Place roast on a rack in a shallow roasting pan; sprinkle with salt. In a small bowl, mix the remaining ingredients; press onto top and sides of roast.

2. Roast 1¾-2¼ hours or until meat reaches desired doneness (for medium-rare, a thermometer should read 135°; medium, 140°; medium well, 145°). Remove roast from oven; tent with foil. Let stand 10 minutes before slicing.

5 OZ. COOKED BEEF: 319 cal., 15g fat (3g sat. fat), 111mg chol., 311mg sod., 7g carb. (0 sugars, 0 fiber), 35g pro. *Diabetic exchanges:* 5 lean meat, 1 fat, ½ starch.

ⓠ GARLIC TILAPIA WITH MUSHROOM RISOTTO

Boxed risotto makes it quick; mushrooms, shallots and cheese make it tasty.
Serve the risotto alongside seasoned fish for a healthy weeknight supper in a hurry.
—*Lynn Moretti, Oconomowoc, WI*

TAKES: 30 min. • **MAKES:** 4 servings

1 pkg. (5½ oz.) Parmesan risotto mix
1 cup sliced fresh mushrooms
¼ cup chopped shallots
1½ lbs. tilapia fillets
1½ tsp. seafood seasoning
4 Tbsp. butter, divided
3 garlic cloves, sliced
¼ cup grated Parmesan cheese

1. Cook risotto according to package directions, adding mushrooms and shallots with the water.

2. Meanwhile, sprinkle tilapia with seafood seasoning. In a large nonstick skillet, heat 2 Tbsp. butter over medium heat. In batches, cook tilapia with garlic until fish just begins to flake easily with a fork, about 5 minutes, turning fillets halfway through cooking.

3. Stir cheese and remaining butter into risotto; remove from heat. Serve with tilapia.

1 SERVING: 432 cal., 18g fat (10g sat. fat), 118mg chol., 964mg sod., 32g carb. (3g sugars, 1g fiber), 39g pro.

ITALIAN WEDDING SOUP SUPPER

Classic Italian wedding soup is a marriage of meatballs, pasta and veggies in a flavorful broth. My family loves it, so I created a stick-to-your-ribs skillet version you can eat with a fork.
—*Patricia Harmon, Baden, PA*

PREP: 25 min. • **COOK:** 15 min. • **MAKES:** 6 servings

2 cups small pasta shells

½ lb. boneless skinless chicken breasts, cut into ¾-in. cubes

2 Tbsp. olive oil, divided

1 medium onion, chopped

1 medium carrot, finely chopped

1 celery rib, chopped

1 pkg. (12 oz.) frozen fully cooked Italian meatballs, thawed

1 can (10¾ oz.) reduced-fat reduced-sodium condensed cream of chicken soup, undiluted

1 pkg. (10 oz.) frozen chopped spinach, thawed and squeezed dry

1 cup reduced-sodium chicken broth

2 tsp. minced fresh thyme or ½ tsp. dried thyme

½ tsp. salt

⅛ tsp. pepper

¾ cup shredded Asiago cheese

1. Cook pasta shells according to package directions. Meanwhile, in a large skillet, saute chicken in 1 Tbsp. oil until no longer pink; remove and keep warm.

2. In the same skillet, saute the chopped onion, carrot and celery in remaining oil until tender. Add meatballs, soup, spinach, broth, thyme, salt, pepper and reserved chicken; cover and cook mixture for 4-6 minutes or until heated through.

3. Drain pasta; stir into skillet. Sprinkle with cheese.

1⅓ CUPS: 473 cal., 24g fat (10g sat. fat), 63mg chol., 1006mg sod., 38g carb. (7g sugars, 4g fiber), 28g pro.

❶ LEMONY TORTELLINI BACON SALAD

Summer meals shouldn't be complicated. We love this simple salad
on warm nights. Adding a glass of iced tea or lemonade on the side is just right.
—*Samantha Vicars, Kenosha, WI*

TAKES: 20 min. • **MAKES:** 4 servings

2 cups frozen cheese tortellini (about 8 oz.)
4 cups fresh broccoli florets
¾ cup mayonnaise
1 Tbsp. balsamic vinegar
2 tsp. lemon juice
¾ tsp. dried oregano
¼ tsp. salt
1 pkg. (5 oz.) spring mix salad greens
4 bacon strips, cooked and crumbled

1. In a large saucepan, cook tortellini according to package directions, adding broccoli during the last 5 minutes of cooking. Meanwhile, in a small bowl, mix mayonnaise, vinegar, lemon juice, oregano and salt.

2. Drain tortellini and broccoli; gently rinse with cold water. Transfer to a large bowl. Add dressing; toss to coat. Serve over salad greens; sprinkle with bacon.

1 CUP SALAD WITH 2 CUPS GREENS: 484 cal., 40g fat (7g sat. fat), 32mg chol., 693mg sod., 21g carb. (3g sugars, 4g fiber), 11g pro.

PIZZA MACARONI & CHEESE

My grandma made this for us once during a visit and I never forgot
how good it was. Since my kids love anything with pepperoni and cheese,
I bake it so they can enjoy it as much as I did.

—*Juli Meyers, Hinesville, GA*

PREP: 30 min. • **BAKE:** 25 min. • **MAKES:** 12 servings

2 pkg. (14 oz. each) deluxe macaroni and cheese dinner mix
½ cup sour cream
1 can (14½ oz.) petite diced tomatoes, drained
1 can (15 oz.) pizza sauce
1 small green pepper, chopped
1 small sweet red pepper, chopped
2 cups shredded Italian cheese blend
2 oz. sliced pepperoni

1. Preheat oven to 350°. Cook macaroni according to package directions for al dente. Drain; return to pan. Stir in contents of cheese packets and sour cream. Transfer to a greased 13x9-in. baking dish.

2. In a small bowl, combine the tomatoes and pizza sauce; drop by spoonfuls over macaroni. Top with peppers, cheese and pepperoni. Bake, uncovered, for 25-30 minutes or until bubbly.

1 CUP: 340 cal., 14g fat (7g sat. fat), 37mg chol., 927mg sod., 37g carb. (5g sugars, 3g fiber), 14g pro.

ⓠ SESAME SHRIMP & RICE

With just a few convenience items, you can put a delightfully flavorful, high-quality meal on the table in minutes.
—*Taste of Home* Test Kitchen

TAKES: 10 min. • **MAKES:** 4 servings

1 pkg. (8.8 oz.) ready-to-serve long grain rice

1 cup fresh or frozen snow peas, thawed

2 green onions, sliced

1 tsp. canola oil

1 lb. cooked medium shrimp, peeled and deveined

1 can (20 oz.) pineapple tidbits, drained

1 can (11 oz.) mandarin oranges, drained

¼ cup sesame ginger salad dressing

2 Tbsp. slivered almonds, toasted

1. Microwave rice according to package directions. Meanwhile, in a large skillet or wok, stir-fry snow peas and onions in oil for 1 minute. Add the shrimp, pineapple, oranges and salad dressing; cook until heated through and vegetables are crisp-tender.

2. Sprinkle with almonds. Serve with rice.

1½ CUPS: 407 cal., 11g fat (1g sat. fat), 172mg chol., 330mg sod., 49g carb. (24g sugars, 3g fiber), 28g pro.

ⓈⒸ SLOW-COOKED CHICKEN A LA KING

When I know I'll be having a busy day with little time to prepare a meal,
I use my slow cooker to make Chicken a la King. It smells so good while it's cooking.
—Eleanor Mielke, Snohomish, WA

PREP: 10 min. • **COOK:** 7½ hours • **MAKES:** 6 servings

1 can (10¾ oz.) reduced-fat reduced-sodium condensed cream of chicken soup, undiluted
3 Tbsp. all-purpose flour
¼ tsp. pepper
Dash cayenne pepper
1 lb. boneless skinless chicken breasts, cubed
1 celery rib, chopped
½ cup chopped green pepper
¼ cup chopped onion
1 pkg. (10 oz.) frozen peas, thawed
2 Tbsp. diced pimientos, drained
Hot cooked rice

In a 3-qt. slow cooker, combine soup, flour, pepper and cayenne until smooth. Stir in chicken, celery, green pepper and onion. Cover and cook on low 7-8 hours or until chicken is no longer pink. Stir in peas and pimientos. Cook 30 minutes longer or until heated through. Serve with rice.

1 CUP: 174 cal., 3g fat (1g sat. fat), 44mg chol., 268mg sod., 16g carb. (6g sugars, 3g fiber), 19g pro. *Diabetic exchanges:* 2 lean meat, 1 starch.

ⓠ GREEK SAUSAGE PITA PIZZAS

I turned my favorite sandwich into a pizza. It's great for lunch or dinner, but don't forget it when you're having a bunch of people over. It makes a great appetizer, too.
—*Marion McNeill, Mayfield Heights, OH*

TAKES: 30 min. • **MAKES:** 4 servings

1 pkg. (19 oz.) Italian sausage links, casings removed
2 garlic cloves, minced
4 whole pita breads
2 plum tomatoes, seeded and chopped
1 medium ripe avocado, peeled and cubed
½ cup crumbled feta cheese
1 small cucumber, sliced
½ cup refrigerated tzatziki sauce

1. Preheat oven to 350°. In a large skillet, cook sausage and garlic over medium heat for 6-8 minutes or until no longer pink, breaking up the sausage into large crumbles; drain.

2. Meanwhile, place pita breads on ungreased baking sheets. Bake 3-4 minutes on each side or until browned and almost crisp.

3. Top pita breads with sausage mixture, tomatoes, avocado and cheese. Bake 3-4 minutes longer or until heated through. Top with cucumbers; drizzle with tzatziki sauce.

1 PIZZA: 632 cal., 40g fat (12g sat. fat), 85mg chol., 1336mg sod., 43g carb. (3g sugars, 5g fiber), 25g pro.

ⓢ HOT PEPPER-BEEF SANDWICHES

If you like your shredded beef with a little kick, then this recipe is for you.
For an even zestier version, add a second jar of jalapenos or use
hot peppers instead of the pepperoncini.
—*Kristen Langmeier, Faribault, MN*

. . . .

PREP: 15 min. • **COOK:** 8 hours • **MAKES:** 12 servings

1   boneless beef chuck roast (4 to 5 lbs.)
2   medium onions, coarsely chopped
1   jar (16 oz.) sliced pepperoncini, undrained
1   jar (8 oz.) pickled jalapeno slices, drained
1   bottle (12 oz.) beer or nonalcoholic beer
1   envelope onion soup mix
5   garlic cloves, minced
½   tsp. pepper
12 kaiser rolls, split
12 slices provolone cheese

1. Cut roast in half; place in a 4- or 5-qt. slow cooker. Add the onions, pepperoncini, jalapenos, beer, soup mix, garlic and pepper.

2. Cover and cook on low for 8-10 hours or until meat is tender.

3. Remove meat. Skim fat from cooking liquid. When cool enough to handle, shred meat with two forks and return to slow cooker; heat through. Serve ½ cup meat mixture on each roll with a slice of cheese.

NOTE: Look for pepperoncini (pickled peppers) in the pickle and olive section of your grocery store.

1 SANDWICH: 534 cal., 23g fat (9g sat. fat), 113mg chol., 1187mg sod., 38g carb. (3g sugars, 3g fiber), 41g pro.

PASTRY-TOPPED SALMON CASSEROLE

This costs about the same as an ordinary chicken potpie, but one bite and you'll be amazed at how much the salmon adds. With cream cheese and the flaky crust, this is no ordinary casserole.
— *Tyler Sherman, Williamsburg, VA*

PREP: 20 min. • **BAKE:** 30 min. • **MAKES:** 6 servings

1 large onion, chopped
5 Tbsp. butter, divided
1 garlic clove, minced
1¼ cups 2% milk
1 pkg. (8 oz.) cream cheese, softened, cubed
2 cups frozen peas and carrots, thawed
1 can (14½ oz.) diced potatoes, drained
2 pouches (6 oz. each) boneless skinless pink salmon, flaked
½ tsp. salt
¼ tsp. pepper
10 sheets phyllo dough (14x9-in. size)

1. Preheat oven to 375°. In a large skillet, saute onion in 2 Tbsp. butter for 5 minutes or until crisp-tender. Add garlic; cook 1 minute. Stir in milk; heat over medium heat until bubbles form around side of pan. Add cheese; stir until cheese is melted. Remove from heat; stir in peas and carrots, potatoes, salmon, salt and pepper.

2. Melt remaining butter; brush some of the butter over the bottom and sides of a 2½-qt. round baking dish. Line with five sheets of phyllo dough. Pour in salmon mixture. Place the remaining sheets of phyllo dough over filling to cover the top. Crimp edges; brush dough with remaining butter.

3. Bake 30-35 minutes or until crust is lightly browned.

1 CUP: 417 cal., 26g fat (16g sat. fat), 90mg chol., 943mg sod., 28g carb. (7g sugars, 3g fiber), 19g pro.

STUFFED ALFREDO PORK CHOPS

Picture this: It's Monday night, dinner's done and you have time to put up your feet. A few ingredients, 15 minutes of prep and hands-free bake time make this smart main dish a busy cook's ideal weeknight meal.
—*Taste of Home* Test Kitchen

PREP: 15 min. • **BAKE:** 25 min. • **MAKES:** 4 servings

1 pkg. (8.8 oz.) ready-to-serve long grain rice
1 pkg. (10 oz.) frozen mixed vegetables
¾ tsp. garlic powder, divided
¾ tsp. Italian seasoning, divided
4 boneless pork loin chops (6 oz. each)
2 Tbsp. butter
1 jar (15 oz.) Alfredo sauce

1. Cook rice and vegetables according to package directions. In a small microwave-safe bowl, combine the vegetables, rice, ½ tsp. garlic powder and ½ tsp. Italian seasoning.

2. Using a sharp knife, cut a pocket in each pork chop. Fill each chop with about ⅓ cup rice mixture; secure with toothpicks if necessary. Set aside remaining rice mixture.

3. In a large skillet, brown chops in butter on both sides. Transfer to a greased 8-in. square baking dish. Cover and bake at 350° for 25-30 minutes or until a thermometer reads 160°.

4. Meanwhile, in a small saucepan, combine the Alfredo sauce and the remaining garlic powder and Italian seasoning; heat through. Cover and microwave remaining rice mixture on high for 30-45 seconds or until heated through. Serve rice with pork chops and sauce mixture.

1 STUFFED PORK CHOP WITH ⅓ CUP RICE MIXTURE AND ⅓ CUP SAUCE: 575 cal., 28g fat (15g sat. fat), 127mg chol., 534mg sod., 38g carb. (2g sugars, 5g fiber), 42g pro.

❶ MANGO & GRILLED CHICKEN SALAD

We live in the hot South, and this awesome fruity chicken salad is a weeknight standout. I buy salad greens and add veggies for color and crunch.
—*Sherry Little, Sherwood, AR*

TAKES: 25 min. • **MAKES:** 4 servings

1 lb. chicken tenderloins
½ tsp. salt
¼ tsp. pepper

SALAD
6 cups torn mixed salad greens
¼ cup raspberry or balsamic vinaigrette
1 medium mango, peeled and cubed
1 cup fresh sugar snap peas, halved lengthwise

1. Toss chicken with salt and pepper. On a lightly oiled grill rack, grill chicken, covered, over medium heat or broil 4 in. from heat 3-4 minutes on each side or until no longer pink. Cut chicken into 1-in. pieces.

2. Divide greens among four plates; drizzle with vinaigrette. Top with chicken, mango and peas; serve immediately.

1 SERVING: 210 cal., 2g fat (0 sat. fat), 56mg chol., 447mg sod., 22g carb. (16g sugars, 4g fiber), 30g pro. *Diabetic exchanges:* 3 lean meat, 2 vegetable, ½ starch, ½ fat.

MEDITERRANEAN BULGUR SPINACH BOWL

You can transform this tasty bowl into an Italian version
with mozzarella, pesto, tomatoes, spinach and basil.
—*Renata Smith, Brookline, MA*

TAKES: 30 min. • **MAKES:** 4 servings

1 cup bulgur
½ tsp. ground cumin
¼ tsp. salt
2 cups water
1 can (15 oz.) chickpeas or garbanzo beans, rinsed and drained
6 oz. fresh baby spinach (about 8 cups)
2 cups cherry tomatoes, halved
1 small red onion, halved and thinly sliced
½ cup crumbled feta cheese
¼ cup hummus
2 Tbsp. chopped fresh mint
2 Tbsp. lemon juice

1. In a 6-qt. stockpot, combine first four ingredients; bring to a boil. Reduce heat; simmer, covered, until tender, 10-12 minutes. Stir in chickpeas; heat through.

2. Remove from heat; stir in baby spinach. Let stand, covered, until spinach is wilted, about 5 minutes. Stir in remaining ingredients. Serve warm or refrigerate and serve cold.

2 CUPS: 311 cal., 7g fat (2g sat. fat), 8mg chol., 521mg sod., 52g carb. (6g sugars, 12g fiber), 14g pro.

✳

TEST KITCHEN TIP

Packed with spinach, tomatoes and feta cheese, this dish supplies all the vitamin A you need in a day.

CHICKEN TAMALE BAKE

When I serve this Mexican-style casserole, everyone ends up with clean plate award. Offer fresh toppings like green onions, tomatoes and avocado.
—*Jennifer Stowell, Deep River, IA*

PREP: 10 min. • **BAKE:** 25 min. + standing • **MAKES:** 8 servings

1 large egg, lightly beaten
1 can (14¾ oz.) cream-style corn
1 pkg. (8½ oz.) cornbread/muffin mix
1 can (4 oz.) chopped green chilies
⅓ cup 2% milk
¼ cup shredded Mexican cheese blend

TOPPING

2 cups coarsely shredded cooked chicken
1 can (10 oz.) enchilada sauce
1 tsp. ground cumin
½ tsp. onion powder
1¾ cups shredded Mexican cheese blend
Chopped green onions, tomatoes and avocado, optional

1. Preheat oven to 400°. In a large bowl, combine the first six ingredients; stir just until dry ingredients are moistened. Transfer to a greased 13x9-in. baking dish. Bake until light golden brown and a toothpick inserted in center comes out clean, 15-18 minutes.

2. In a large skillet, combine chicken, enchilada sauce, cumin and onion powder; bring to a boil, stirring occasionally. Reduce heat; simmer, uncovered, for 5 minutes. Spread over cornbread layer; sprinkle with cheese.

3. Bake until cheese is melted, 10-12 minutes longer. Let stand 10 minutes before serving. If desired, top with green onions, tomatoes and avocado.

1 PIECE: 364 cal., 17g fat (7g sat. fat), 81mg chol., 851mg sod., 35g carb. (9g sugars, 4g fiber), 21g pro.

ⓢ SAUCY CHICKEN & TORTELLINI

This heartwarming dish is something I threw together years ago for my oldest daughter. When she's having a rough day, I put on the slow cooker and prepare this special recipe.
—Mary Morgan, Dallas, TX

. . . .

PREP: 10 min. • **COOK:** 6¼ hours • **MAKES:** 8 servings

1½ lbs. boneless skinless chicken breasts, cut into 1-in. cubes
½ lb. sliced fresh mushrooms
1 large onion, chopped
1 medium sweet red pepper, cut into ½-in. pieces
1 medium green pepper, cut into ½-in. pieces
1 can (2¼ oz.) sliced ripe olives, drained
1 jar (24 oz.) marinara sauce
1 jar (15 oz.) Alfredo sauce
2 pkg. (9 oz. each) refrigerated cheese tortellini
   Grated Parmesan cheese, optional
   Torn fresh basil, optional

1. In a 5-qt. slow cooker, combine the first seven ingredients. Cook, covered, on low until chicken is tender, 6-8 hours.

2. Stir in Alfredo sauce and tortellini. Cook, covered, until tortellini is tender, 15-20 minutes. If desired, top with Parmesan cheese and basil.

FREEZE OPTION: Place chicken and vegetables in freezer containers; top with sauce. Cool and freeze. To use, partially thaw in the refrigerator overnight. Microwave, covered, on high in a microwave-safe dish until heated through, stirring gently and adding a little water if necessary.

1¼ CUPS: 437 cal., 15g fat (7g sat. fat), 91mg chol., 922mg sod., 44g carb. (8g sugars, 5g fiber), 31g pro.

EASY CHEDDAR CHICKEN POTPIE

My kids love chicken potpie, and I really like that this is so quick and easy to put together with frozen veggies and store-bought gravy. To make it even simpler, my friend and I decided to top it with a biscuit crust instead of homemade pastry. It's delicious!
—*Linda Drees, Palestine, TX*

PREP: 20 min. • **BAKE:** 25 min. • **MAKES:** 6 servings

1 pkg. (16 oz.) frozen vegetables for stew, thawed and coarsely chopped

1 jar (12 oz.) chicken gravy

2 cups shredded cheddar cheese

2 cups cubed cooked chicken

2 cups biscuit/baking mix

1 tsp. minced fresh or ¼ tsp. dried thyme

2 large eggs

¼ cup 2% milk

1. Combine vegetables and gravy in a large saucepan. Bring to a boil. Reduce heat; stir in cheese and chicken. Cook and stir until the cheese is melted. Pour into a greased 11x7-in. baking dish.

2. Combine biscuit mix and thyme in a small bowl. In another small bowl, whisk eggs and milk; stir into the dry ingredients just until moistened. Drop by tablespoonfuls over chicken mixture; spread gently.

3. Bake, uncovered, at 375° for 23-27 minutes or until golden brown. Let stand for 5 minutes before serving.

1 SERVING: 481 cal., 22g fat (10g sat. fat), 146mg chol., 977mg sod., 41g carb. (3g sugars, 2g fiber), 29g pro.

MAKEOVER SWISS CHICKEN SUPREME

Even though this family-favorite recipe is slimmed down, it's still supreme!
—*Stephanie Bell, Kaysville, UT*

PREP: 15 min. • **BAKE:** 30 min. • **MAKES:** 4 servings

4 boneless skinless chicken breast halves (4 oz. each)

1 Tbsp. dried minced onion

½ tsp. garlic powder

¼ tsp. salt

⅛ tsp. pepper

4 slices (¾ oz. each) reduced-fat Swiss cheese

1 can (10¾ oz.) reduced-fat reduced-sodium condensed cream of chicken soup, undiluted

⅓ cup reduced-fat sour cream

½ cup fat-free milk

⅓ cup crushed reduced-fat Ritz crackers (about 8 crackers)

1 tsp. butter, melted

1. Place the chicken in a 13x9-in. baking dish coated with cooking spray. Sprinkle with minced onion, garlic powder, salt and pepper. Top each with a slice of cheese.

2. In a small bowl, combine the soup, sour cream and milk; pour over chicken. Toss the cracker crumbs and butter; sprinkle over chicken. Bake, uncovered, at 350° for 30-40 minutes or until a thermometer reads 170°.

1 CHICKEN BREAST HALF: 291 cal., 11g fat (5g sat. fat), 89mg chol., 587mg sod., 14g carb. (5g sugars, 0 fiber), 34g pro. *Diabetic exchanges:* 3 lean meat, 1 starch, 1 fat.

**EASY NUTELLA
CHEESECAKE, 226**

CHAPTER 6

SWEET & SIMPLE FINALES

Here's hoping you saved room for dessert, because with these delicacies, we saved the best for last!

SC SLOW COOKER CHERRY BUCKLE

I saw this recipe on a cooking show and came up with my own version. When the amazing aroma of this homey dessert drifts around the house, it's hard not to take a peek inside.
—*Sherri Melotik, Oak Creek, WI*

PREP: 10 min. • **COOK:** 3 hours • **MAKES:** 8 servings

2 cans (15 oz. each) sliced pears, drained
1 can (21 oz.) cherry pie filling
¼ tsp. almond extract
1 pkg. yellow cake mix (regular size)
¼ cup old-fashioned oats
¼ cup sliced almonds
1 Tbsp. brown sugar
½ cup butter, melted
  Vanilla ice cream, optional

1. In a greased 5-qt. slow cooker, combine pears and pie filling; stir in extract. In a large bowl, combine cake mix, oats, almonds and brown sugar; stir in melted butter. Sprinkle over fruit.

2. Cook, covered, on low 3-4 hours or until topping is golden brown. If desired, serve with ice cream.

1 SERVING: 324 cal., 13g fat (8g sat. fat), 31mg chol., 152mg sod., 49g carb. (24g sugars, 2g fiber), 1g pro.

WHOOPIE COOKIES

I don't always have time to make whoopie pies from scratch, so I tweaked a cake mix recipe to create these. Try a bit of peanut butter in the filling, too.
—*Nundi Harris, Las Vegas, NV*

PREP: 20 min. + chilling • **BAKE:** 10 min./batch + cooling • **MAKES:** 1½ dozen

1 pkg. devil's food cake mix (regular size)
¼ cup butter, softened
2 large eggs
1 jar (7 oz.) marshmallow creme
4 oz. cream cheese, softened

1. In a large bowl, beat cake mix and butter until well combined. Beat in eggs. Shape into 1-in. balls. Place 2 in. apart on ungreased baking sheets.

2. Bake at 350° for 7-9 minutes or until tops are cracked. Cool for 2 minutes before removing to wire racks to cool completely.

3. In a large bowl, beat marshmallow creme and cream cheese until blended (do not overbeat). Spread filling on the bottoms of half of the cookies. Top with remaining cookies. Chill for 1-2 hours or until filling is set.

1 SANDWICH COOKIE: 152 cal., 5g fat (3g sat. fat), 28mg chol., 206mg sod., 25g carb. (16g sugars, 1g fiber), 2g pro.

FROZEN PEANUT BUTTER & CHOCOLATE TERRINE

This terrine can be made ahead of time and stored in the freezer.
When served, it cuts easily and has that "wow" factor with the
lovely layers of banana, peanut butter and chocolate.
—*Jennifer Jackson, Keller, TX*

PREP: 30 min. + freezing • **MAKES:** 12 servings

15 Nutter Butter cookies, crushed (about 2 cups)
1 carton (16 oz.) mascarpone cheese
1 cup sugar
2 tsp. vanilla extract
1 carton (8 oz.) frozen whipped topping, thawed
1 medium banana, sliced
1 cup semisweet chocolate chips, melted and cooled slightly
1 Tbsp. baking cocoa
1 cup chunky peanut butter

1. Line a 9x5-in. loaf pan with plastic wrap, letting edges extend up all sides. Sprinkle with a third of the crushed cookies.

2. In a large bowl, mix mascarpone cheese, sugar and vanilla; fold in whipped topping. Divide mixture evenly among three bowls.

3. To one portion, fold in sliced banana; add to loaf pan, spreading evenly. Repeat cookie layer. To a second portion, stir in melted chocolate and cocoa; add to loaf pan. Sprinkle with remaining cookies. To third portion, stir in peanut butter. Spread over top.

4. Freeze, covered, until firm, at least 5 hours. To serve, invert terrine onto a platter; remove plastic wrap. Cut into slices.

1 SLICE: 568 cal., 39g fat (18g sat. fat), 47mg chol., 190mg sod., 49g carb. (38g sugars, 3g fiber), 10g pro.

TEST KITCHEN TIP

Homemade whipped cream can be substituted for whipped topping. Beat 1¾ cups heavy whipping cream with 2-3 Tbsp. confectioners' sugar until soft peaks form.

BERRY DREAM CAKE

I use cherry gelatin to give cake mix an eye-catching marbled effect. It's so festive-looking. Top it with whatever fruit you like!
—*Margaret McNeil, Germantown, TN*

PREP: 15 min. + chilling • **BAKE:** 30 min. + cooling • **MAKES:** 15 servings

1 pkg. white cake mix (regular size)
1½ cups boiling water
1 pkg. (3 oz.) cherry gelatin
1 pkg. (8 oz.) cream cheese, softened
2 cups whipped topping
4 cups fresh strawberries, coarsely chopped

1. Prepare and bake cake batter according to package directions, using a greased 13x9-in. baking pan.

2. In a small bowl, add boiling water to gelatin; stir 2 minutes to completely dissolve. Cool cake on a wire rack 3-5 minutes. Using a wooden skewer, pierce holes in top of cake to within 1 in. of edge, twisting skewer gently to make slightly larger holes. Gradually pour gelatin over cake, being careful to fill each hole. Cool 15 minutes. Refrigerate, covered, 30 minutes.

3. In a large bowl, beat cream cheese until fluffy. Fold in whipped topping. Carefully spread over cake. Top with strawberries. Cover and refrigerate for at least 2 hours before serving.

1 PIECE: 306 cal., 16g fat (6g sat. fat), 54mg chol., 315mg sod., 37g carb. (22g sugars, 1g fiber), 5g pro.

EASY NUTELLA CHEESECAKE

A creamy chocolate-hazelnut spread tops a crust made of crushed Oreo cookies to make this irresistible baked cheesecake.
—*Nick Iverson, Denver, CO*

PREP: 35 min. • **BAKE:** 1¼ hour + chilling • **MAKES:** 16 servings

2½ cups lightly crushed Oreo cookies (about 24 cookies)
¼ cup sugar
¼ cup butter, melted

FILLING

4 pkg. (8 oz. each) cream cheese, softened
½ cup sugar
2 jars (26½ oz. each) Nutella
1 cup heavy whipping cream
1 tsp. salt
4 large eggs, lightly beaten
½ cup chopped, toasted hazelnuts

TEST KITCHEN TIP

Don't overbeat the eggs. Mixing too much air into them will make the cheesecake puff up in the oven, then collapse and crack once it's out.

1. Preheat oven to 325°. Pulse cookies and sugar in a food processor until fine crumbs form. Continue processing while gradually adding butter in a steady stream. Press mixture onto the bottom of a greased 10x3-in. springform pan. Securely wrap bottom and sides of springform in a double thickness of heavy-duty foil (about 18 in. square).

2. For filling, beat together cream cheese and sugar until smooth. Beat in Nutella, cream and salt. Add eggs; beat on low speed just until blended. Pour over crust.

3. Bake until a thermometer inserted in center reads 160°, about 1¼ hours. Cool 1¼ hours on a wire rack. Refrigerate cheesecake overnight, covering when completely cooled.

4. Gently loosen sides from pan with a knife; remove rim. Top cheesecake with chopped hazelnuts.

1 SLICE: 900 cal., 62g fat (22g sat. fat), 129mg chol., 478mg sod., 84g carb. (71g sugars, 4g fiber), 12g pro.

COCONUT POPPY SEED CAKE

I'm known for my coconut cake and it is definitely one of my most-requested desserts. You can change it up by using different cake mixes and pudding flavors.
—*Gail Cayce, Wautoma, WI*

PREP: 15 min. • **BAKE:** 20 min. + cooling • **MAKES:** 24 servings

1 pkg. white cake mix (regular size)
½ cup sweetened shredded coconut
¼ cup poppy seeds
3½ cups cold whole milk
1 tsp. coconut extract
2 pkg. (3.4 oz. each) instant vanilla pudding mix
1 carton (8 oz.) frozen whipped topping, thawed
⅓ cup sweetened shredded coconut, toasted, optional

1. Prepare cake according to package directions, adding coconut and poppy seeds to batter.

2. Pour into a greased 13x9-in. baking pan. Bake at 350° for 20-25 minutes or until a toothpick inserted in the center comes out clean. Cool completely.

3. In a large bowl, whisk the milk, extract and pudding mixes for 2 minutes. Let stand for 2 minutes or until soft-set. Spread over the cake. Spread with whipped topping. Sprinkle with toasted coconut if desired.

1 PIECE: 211 cal., 9g fat (4g sat. fat), 27mg chol., 231mg sod., 30g carb. (20g sugars, 1g fiber), 3g pro.

TOFFEE BROWNIE TRIFLE

This decadent combination of pantry items is a terrific way to dress up a brownie mix. Try it with other flavors of pudding or substitute your favorite candy bar. It tastes great with low-fat and sugar-free products, too.
—*Wendy Bennett, Sioux Falls, SD*

PREP: 20 min. • **BAKE:** 25 min. + cooling • **MAKES:** 16 servings

1 pkg. fudge brownie mix (13x9-in. pan size)

2½ cups cold whole milk

1 pkg. (3.4 oz.) instant cheesecake or vanilla pudding mix

1 pkg. (3.3 oz.) instant white chocolate pudding mix

1 carton (8 oz.) frozen whipped topping, thawed

2 Heath candy bars (1.4 oz. each), chopped

1. Prepare and bake brownies according to package directions for cake-like brownies, using a greased 13x9-in. baking pan. Cool completely on a wire rack.

2. In a large bowl, beat milk and pudding mixes on low speed for 2 minutes. Let stand for 2 minutes or until soft-set. Fold in whipped topping.

3. Cut the brownies into 1-in. cubes; place half in a 3-qt. glass trifle bowl or serving dish. Cover with half of the pudding. Repeat layers. Sprinkle with chopped candy bars. Refrigerate leftovers.

1 SERVING: 265 cal., 8g fat (4g sat. fat), 7mg chol., 329mg sod., 45g carb. (31g sugars, 1g fiber), 3g pro.

OLD-FASHIONED OATMEAL RAISIN COOKIES

I've been making these cookies for nearly 30 years. The spice cake mix provides a delicious backdrop to the oats and raisins. They are an all-time favorite with my family.
—*Nancy Horton, Greenbrier, TN*

PREP: 10 min. • **BAKE:** 10 min./batch • **MAKES:** 7 dozen

¾ cup canola oil
¼ cup packed brown sugar
2 large eggs
½ cup 2% milk
1 pkg. spice cake mix (regular size)
2 cups old-fashioned oats
2½ cups raisins
1 cup chopped pecans

1. In a large bowl, beat oil and brown sugar until blended. Beat in eggs, then milk. Combine cake mix and oats; gradually add to brown sugar mixture and mix well. Fold in raisins and pecans.

2. Drop by tablespoonfuls 2 in. apart onto greased baking sheets. Bake at 350° for 10-12 minutes or until golden brown. Cool for 1 minute before removing to wire racks.

1 COOKIE: 79 cal., 4g fat (1g sat. fat), 7mg chol., 50mg sod., 10g carb. (6g sugars, 1g fiber), 1g pro.

LAYERED CANDY CANE DESSERT

This fabulous dessert has the magical flavor of candy canes plus the bonus of an Oreo cookie crust. And it looks like a winter wonderland!
—*Dawn Kreuser, Green Bay, WI*

PREP: 25 min. + chilling • **MAKES:** 24 servings

1 pkg. (14.3 oz.) Oreo cookies
6 Tbsp. butter, melted
1 pkg. (8 oz.) cream cheese, softened
¼ cup sugar
2 Tbsp. 2% milk
1 carton (12 oz.) frozen whipped topping, thawed, divided
¾ cup crushed candy canes (about 7 regular size), divided
2 pkg. (3.3 oz. each) instant white chocolate pudding mix
2¾ cups cold 2% milk

1. Pulse cookies in a food processor until fine crumbs form. Add melted butter; pulse just until combined. Press onto bottom of a 13x9-in. dish. Refrigerate while preparing filling.

2. Beat cream cheese, sugar and milk until smooth. Fold in 1 cup whipped topping and ½ cup crushed candies. Spread over crust.

3. Whisk pudding mix and milk 2 minutes; spread over cream cheese layer. Spread with remaining whipped topping. Refrigerate, covered, 4 hours. Sprinkle with remaining candies just before serving.

1 PIECE: 251 cal., 13g fat (7g sat. fat), 20mg chol., 250mg sod., 32g carb. (25g sugars, 1g fiber), 2g pro.

CAN'T LEAVE ALONE BARS

I bring these treats to church meetings, potlucks and housewarming parties. I often make a double batch so we can enjoy some at home, too.
—*Kimberly Biel, Java, SD*

PREP: 20 min. • **BAKE:** 20 min. + cooling • **MAKES:** 3 dozen

1 pkg. white cake mix (regular size)
2 large eggs
⅓ cup canola oil
1 can (14 oz.) sweetened condensed milk
1 cup semisweet chocolate chips
¼ cup butter, cubed

1. Preheat oven to 350°. In a large bowl, combine the cake mix, eggs and oil. Press two-thirds of the mixture into a greased 13x9-in. baking pan. Set remaining cake mixture aside.

2. In a microwave-safe bowl, combine the milk, chocolate chips and butter. Microwave, uncovered, until chips and butter are melted; stir until smooth. Pour over crust.

3. Drop teaspoonfuls of remaining cake mixture over top. Bake 20-25 minutes or until lightly browned. Cool before cutting.

1 SERVING: 152 cal., 7g fat (3g sat. fat), 19mg chol., 122mg sod., 20g carb. (15g sugars, 0 fiber), 2g pro.

BANANA CREAM CHOCOLATE TRUFFLES

This truffle recipe was created from ripe bananas and my imagination, and the outcome blew my family and friends away! I don't particularly like bananas, but I could eat these truffles all day long.
—*Michele Lassuy, Orlando, FL*

PREP: 35 min. + freezing • **MAKES:** 4 dozen

1 pkg. (14.3 oz.) Golden Oreo cookies

1 pkg. (8 oz.) cream cheese, softened

2 tsp. banana extract

⅓ cup mashed ripe banana

1 lb. milk chocolate candy coating, melted

Dried banana chips, coarsely crushed

1. Pulse cookies in a food processor until fine crumbs form. In a bowl, beat cream cheese and extract until blended. Beat in banana. Stir in cookie crumbs. Freeze, covered, until firm enough to shape, about 2 hours.

2. Shape mixture into 1-in. balls. Dip cookie balls in candy coating; place on waxed paper-lined baking sheets. Top immediately with banana chips.

3. Refrigerate until set, about 30 minutes. Store in a covered container in the refrigerator.

1 TRUFFLE: 110 cal., 6g fat (4g sat. fat), 5mg chol., 45mg sod., 13g carb. (9g sugars, 0 fiber), 1g pro.

FRESH RASPBERRY ICEBOX CAKE

Layered icebox cakes are so fun because they look impressive but couldn't be easier. Fresh raspberries make this one really special. Use Anna's Ginger Thins to get the scalloped edges, or regular gingersnaps if those are not available.
—*Elisabeth Larsen, Pleasant Grove, UT*

PREP: 25 min. + chilling • **MAKES:** 12 servings

1 carton (8 oz.) mascarpone cheese
3 cups cold heavy whipping cream
2 Tbsp. sugar
2 Tbsp. grated lemon zest (about 2 lemons)
2 pkg. (5¼ oz. each) thin ginger cookies
5 cups fresh raspberries (about 20 oz.), divided

1. Stir mascarpone; let stand at room temperature 30 minutes. Meanwhile, beat cream until it begins to thicken. Add sugar; beat until soft peaks form. Reserve ½ cup cream; cover and refrigerate. Add lemon zest and mascarpone to remaining whipped cream; beat until stiff peaks form, 30-60 seconds.

2. On a serving plate, spread ½ cup of the cream mixture in a 7-in.-diameter circle. Arrange six cookies in a circle on top of the cream, placing a seventh cookie in the center. Gently fold 4 cups of raspberries into remaining cream mixture. Spoon about 1 cup raspberry cream mixture over the cookies. Repeat layers six times, ending with cookies (there will be eight cookie layers in all). Spread reserved whipped cream over cookies; top with remaining raspberries. Refrigerate, covered, overnight.

1 SLICE: 421 cal., 35g fat (21g sat. fat), 91mg chol., 132mg sod., 25g carb. (13g sugars, 3g fiber), 4g pro.

ⓈⒸ CARIBBEAN BREAD PUDDING

A completely unexpected slow cooker dessert, it's moist and sweet with plump, juicy raisins and the wonderful tropical flavors of pineapple and coconut.
—*Elizabeth Doss, California City, CA*

PREP: 30 min. • **COOK:** 4 hours • **MAKES:** 16 servings

1 cup raisins

1 can (8 oz.) crushed pineapple, undrained

2 large firm bananas, halved

1 can (12 oz.) evaporated milk

1 can (10 oz.) frozen non-alcoholic pina colada mix

1 can (6 oz.) unsweetened pineapple juice

3 large eggs

½ cup cream of coconut

¼ cup light rum, optional

1 loaf (1 lb.) French bread, cut into 1-in. cubes

Whipped cream and maraschino cherries, optional

1. In a small bowl, combine raisins and pineapple; set aside. In a blender, combine the bananas, milk, pina colada mix, pineapple juice, eggs, cream of coconut and, if desired, rum. Cover and process until smooth.

2. Place two-thirds of the bread in a greased 6-qt. slow cooker. Top with 1 cup raisin mixture. Layer with remaining bread and raisin mixture. Pour banana mixture over the top. Cover and cook on low for 4-5 hours or until a knife inserted in the center comes out clean. Serve warm with whipped cream and cherries if desired.

¾ CUP: 245 cal., 4g fat (3g sat. fat), 7mg chol., 215mg sod., 46g carb. (27g sugars, 2g fiber), 5g pro.

CHOCOLATE PEANUT BUTTER COOKIES

It's a snap to make a batch of tasty cookies using this recipe. My husband and son gobble them up.
—*Mary Pulyer, Port St. Lucie, FL*

PREP: 10 min. • **BAKE:** 10 min./batch • **MAKES:** 4 dozen

1 pkg. devil's food cake mix (regular size)
2 large eggs
⅓ cup canola oil
1 pkg. (10 oz.) peanut butter chips

TEST KITCHEN TIP

For a cute Halloween-themed variation, use Reese's Pieces instead of peanut butter chips.

1. In a bowl, beat cake mix, eggs and oil (batter will be very stiff). Stir in chips.

2. Roll into 1-in. balls. Place on lightly greased baking sheets; flatten slightly. Bake at 350° for 10 minutes or until a slight indentation remains when lightly touched. Cool on pans for 2 minutes before removing to wire racks.

2 COOKIES: 184 cal., 9g fat (3g sat. fat), 18mg chol., 205mg sod., 22g carb. (12g sugars, 2g fiber), 4g pro.

FROZEN STRAWBERRY DESSERT

When I'm planning party menus, I appreciate dessert recipes like this; you can make and freeze it up to two weeks before serving. A refreshing slice is welcome after a big meal.
—*Cassie Alexander, Muncie, IN*

PREP: 25 min. + freezing • **MAKES:** 15 servings

1¼ cups crushed pretzels
¼ cup sugar
½ cup butter, melted

FILLING
1 can (14 oz.) sweetened condensed milk
½ cup thawed non-alcoholic strawberry daiquiri mix
1 pkg. (8 oz.) cream cheese, softened
1 container (16 oz.) frozen sweetened sliced strawberries, thawed
1 carton (8 oz.) frozen whipped topping, thawed

SAUCE
1 container (16 oz.) frozen sweetened sliced strawberries, thawed and undrained

1. In a small bowl, combine the pretzels, sugar and butter. Press onto the bottom of a greased 11x7-in. dish. Refrigerate for 30 minutes.

2. For filling, in a large bowl, combine milk and daiquiri mix. Beat in the cream cheese until smooth. Stir in the strawberries; fold in whipped topping. Pour over crust (dish will be full). Freeze for 4 hours before serving.

3. For sauce, puree thawed undrained strawberries in a food processor or blender. Strain through a fine sieve. Drizzle over top.

TO MAKE AHEAD: This dessert can be made and stored in the freezer for two weeks before serving.

1 PIECE: 349 cal., 17g fat (11g sat. fat), 41mg chol., 240mg sod., 48g carb. (40g sugars, 1g fiber), 4g pro.

CREAM-FILLED CUPCAKES

These chocolate cupcakes have a fun filling and shiny chocolate frosting that make them extra special. They always disappear in a flash!
—*Kathy Kittell, Lenexa, KS*

PREP: 20 min. • **BAKE:** 15 min. + cooling • **MAKES:** 2 dozen

1 pkg. devil's food cake mix (regular size)
2 tsp. hot water
¼ tsp. salt
1 jar (7 oz.) marshmallow creme
½ cup shortening
⅓ cup confectioners' sugar
½ tsp. vanilla extract

GANACHE FROSTING
1 cup semisweet chocolate chips
¾ cup heavy whipping cream

1. Prepare and bake cake batter according to package directions, using paper-lined muffin cups. Cool cupcakes for 5 minutes before removing from pans to wire racks to cool completely.

2. For filling, in a small bowl, combine water and salt until salt is dissolved. Cool. In a small bowl, beat the marshmallow creme, shortening, confectioners' sugar and vanilla until light and fluffy; beat in salt mixture.

3. Cut a small hole in the corner of a plastic or pastry bag; insert round pastry tip. Fill the bag with cream filling. Push the tip through the bottom of paper liner to fill each cupcake.

4. Place chocolate chips in a small bowl. In a small saucepan, bring the cream just to a boil. Pour over chocolate; whisk until smooth. Stirring occasionally, cool ganache to room temperature or until it reaches a dipping consistency.

5. Dip cupcake tops in ganache; chill for 20 minutes or until set. Store in the refrigerator.

1 CUPCAKE: 262 cal., 15g fat (5g sat. fat), 32mg chol., 223mg sod., 29g carb. (20g sugars, 1g fiber), 2g pro.

LEMONADE ICEBOX PIE

You will detect a definite lemonade flavor in this refreshing pie. High and fluffy, this dessert has a creamy smooth consistency that we really appreciate. It's the dessert that comes to mind immediately when I put together my favorite summer meal.
—*Cheryl Wilt, Eglon, WV*

PREP: 15 min. + chilling • **MAKES:** 8 servings

1 pkg. (8 oz.) cream cheese, softened
1 can (14 oz.) sweetened condensed milk
¾ cup thawed lemonade concentrate
1 carton (8 oz.) frozen whipped topping, thawed
  Yellow food coloring, optional
1 graham cracker crust (9 in.)

In a large bowl, beat cream cheese and milk until smooth. Beat in lemonade concentrate. Fold in whipped topping and, if desired, food coloring. Pour into crust. Cover and refrigerate until set.

1 PIECE: 491 cal., 24g fat (15g sat. fat), 48mg chol., 269mg sod., 61g carb. (52g sugars, 0 fiber), 7g pro.

ORANGE ICEBOX PIE: Substitute ¾ cup thawed orange juice concentrate for the lemonade, add ½ tsp. grated orange zest and omit food coloring.

CREAMY PINEAPPLE PIE: Substitute 1 can (8 oz.) crushed, undrained pineapple and ¼ cup lemon juice for lemonade. Omit food coloring.

COOL LIME PIE: Substitute ¾ cup thawed limeade concentrate for lemonade and use green food coloring instead of yellow.

SHORTCUT COCONUT-PECAN CHOCOLATE TASSIES

You can garnish these cookies with pecan halves or a couple of chocolate chips before baking, or drizzle with a little melted chocolate after taking them out of the oven.
—*Deb Villenauve, Krakow, WI*

PREP: 25 min. • **BAKE:** 10 min./batch + cooling • **MAKES:** 3 dozen

1 pkg. chocolate cake mix (regular size)
½ cup quick-cooking oats
1 large egg, lightly beaten
6 Tbsp. butter, melted and cooled slightly
¾ cup coconut-pecan frosting
Pecan halves or melted semisweet chocolate, optional

1. Preheat oven to 350°. Mix cake mix and oats; stir in egg and melted butter. Shape mixture into 1-in. balls. Press onto bottom and up sides of greased mini muffin cups.

2. Bake just until set, 8-10 minutes. Cool slightly before removing to wire racks; cool completely.

3. Top each with about 1 tsp. frosting. If desired, top with pecans or drizzle with melted chocolate.

1 TASSIE: 94 cal., 4g fat (2g sat. fat), 10mg chol., 105mg sod., 13g carb. (8g sugars, 1g fiber), 1g pro.

TEST KITCHEN TIP

If you like German chocolate cake, you'll love these bite-sized versions. It's a little tricky to tell when the cake cups are done baking. When they are set, they look more matte than glossy.

RECIPE INDEX